SHARING TIME
FAMILY TIME
ANYTIME

SHARING TIME FAMILY TIME ANYTIME

Beth Lefgren and Jennifer Jackson

Bookcraft
Salt Lake City, Utah

Library of Congress Catalog Card Number: 92-73807
ISBN 0-88494-846-3

Third Printing, 1993

Printed in the United States of America

Contents

1. Lesson Activities

2. Making Reusable Visuals

3. Music Time Ideas

Preface

Yes! This book was written for the very special needs of Primary Sharing Time. No! Please don't limit your use of the book to Primary only. The ideas and activities have been designed to be flexible, enabling you to successfully use them in family home evenings or anytime you have a teaching opportunity.

The sections of this book were designed to give ideas and help in three areas of teaching: activities and lessons, making and using reusable visual aids, and music ideas and helps.

Lesson Activities. Use this section to discover new and creative ways to teach a wide variety of subjects. Nearly fifty topics are addressed to fit a wide range of teaching circumstances.

Making Reusable Visuals. This section will prove to be invaluable, as it offers easy, inexpensive ideas for visual aids that will make your lessons stimulating and memorable.

Music Time Ideas. Here you will find a selection of games and activities that will increase participation, enthusiasm, and mastery in singing situations. These activities will quickly become favorites!

In those lessons that utilize pictures, brief descriptions of the pictures along with their library numbers have been given so that you can find them easily in your meetinghouse library. Note that the numbers for these pictures were changed slightly in 1991, the letters *OQ* being replaced by the numbers *62* in the library filing system. (Thus, picture OQ002, for example, was changed to 62002.) Since some meetinghouse libraries have not yet adopted the newer numbering system, and since the change from OQ to 62 is really minor, we've chosen to use the pre-1991 numbers. Of course, other Church-related pictures available to you can be substituted for any of those we suggest.

We hope you will feel that *Sharing Time, Family Time, Anytime* has reached its goal by offering you a vast range of resources. Games, stories, scripture references, music selections, object lessons, and visual aids are only the beginning.

Teaching children will be easier, more interesting, and more successful as you use the ideas presented in this book. You will experience the true payoff of your efforts as students become attentive and excited and your lessons begin to make an impact on their lives. There is no greater reward than this.

How to Use the Lesson Activities Section

The lesson activities section of this book contains a wide variety of complete lessons. We have endeavored to offer a large selection of topics to meet your varied needs. To aid in the use of these lessons, the following suggestions may be helpful:

1. Notice that the subjects are arranged in alphabetical order for ease in browsing and locating. Many topics can be interchanged. For example, a lesson on choosing the right might easily be used for the subject of repentance. You will find the possibilities are limitless as you use your personal creativity and inspiration.

2. Each lesson contains many ideas and activities. Keep in mind that you don't have to use every part of every idea. You can easily individualize these lessons by selecting the material which best suits your age group, time allowance, or other special needs.

3. Unless otherwise indicated, songs suggested are from *Children's Songbook*, 1989.

4. Scripture references are used often during the lessons. When children see you refer to actual scriptures for these references as opposed to a piece of paper or even a mental note, it will serve as a powerful example.

5. Correlation and cooperation is vital for a well-rounded presentation. Communicate your lesson plan and desired outcome to any individuals involved—music leaders, teachers, or assistants. When all concerned parties plan for a mutual goal, the lesson will have a greater impact.

6. Prayerfully ready your lesson in advance. This gives you time to ponder and prepare for its presentation. By listening to the Spirit, you will be able to perceive individual needs.

7. Your greatest resource is your students. Try to involve as many members of your group as possible; the lesson becomes more meaningful and memorable if they take an active part.

We know that as you apply these guidelines you will experience wonderful success. We have.

1

Lesson Activities

Children of God

Purpose

To help the children understand that they are sons and daughters of a loving Heavenly Father.

Preparation

Prepare pictures of animal babies and animal parents for matching.
Prepare a display area by mounting the pictures of the baby animals. Leave a space underneath or to the side for its "parent" match.

Application

Activity: Select a "parent" picture and ask a child to find its matching "baby" picture. Repeat until all the pictures are matched.

Discussion: Tell the children that a baby will grow up to be like its parents. Just as a foal will someday grow to look like a horse, children grow until they are as tall and know as much as their parents. Remind them that they have another parent that they want to be like. Ask if anyone knows who that is. (Heavenly Father.) Tell the children that Heavenly Father is the father of our spirits and that we lived with him before we were born to our earthly parents. Explain that just as we will someday be more like our moms and dads, we can become like Heavenly Father too.

Object Lesson: Cut an apple in half widthwise. Show it to the children. Explain that inside every apple there is a five-sided star that holds seeds. Tell the children that it doesn't matter what condition the outside of the apple is in, the star and seeds are still there.
   Explain that we are like the apple. Each of us has the ability to become like Heavenly Father because we are his children. We can use our "seeds," plant them, nourish them, and help them grow so that someday we can be like Heavenly Father.

Chalkboard Discussion: What can we do to become like Heavenly Father? List the children's responses on the chalkboard. (Pray, learn what to do, read scriptures, keep the commandments, love others, etc.) Tell the children that Heavenly Father wants them to be like him because he loves them and wants them to always be happy.

Singing Time Suggestions

"I Lived in Heaven," 4
"I Am a Child of God," 2

Conclusion

Show the children the apple and remind them that they can be like Heavenly Father.

Choices

Purpose

To help the children understand that by using their knowledge they can make good choices every day.

l

Preparation

Prepare to tell and discuss each story.

Print the last part of Helaman 14:30 on a lineboard. ("For behold, ye are free; ye are permitted to act for yourselves; for behold, God hath given unto you a knowledge and he hath made you free.")

Application

Choral Reading and Discussion: Read the scripture on the lineboard as a group.

What does *permitted* mean? (To be allowed.)

What does the word *knowledge* mean? (Something that you learn.)

Who gives us knowledge? (School, family, church.)

Explain that because Heavenly Father loves us, he helps us learn ideas, then gives us chances to act or choose for ourselves.

Activity: Use the following stories (or others of your own choosing) to help the children understand that any situation has many choices available with it. Use discussion to allow the children to come up with as many good choices as they can.

1. Sally would like a candy bar but doesn't have enough money to pay for it. It's been a long time since she's had a candy bar. Everyone around her in the store is very busy and she knows that no one will notice if she takes it without paying. What choices does she have? (Ask her parents if she can work for the extra money; buy a lower-priced candy bar; etc.)

2. Tommy, Sam, and Craig are playing tag at school. They see Jared sitting all alone under the tree. They think it would be nice to invite him to play

5

with them but they would have to stop their own game to get him. What are their choices? (Send one boy over to invite him; finish the game early and go talk with Jared, then invite him to play next time; etc.)

3. Mother has not been happy today. Johnny can tell that something is bothering her, but she just yelled at him for something he didn't do. It would be very easy to stay angry. What are his choices? (Take time out to tell his mother he loves her; pray for help to not be angry; etc.)

4. Tammy's best friend is playing at Hillary's house. Her friend said that she wanted to come to Tammy's house to play and now Tammy can't understand why she wasn't called first. Tammy feels hurt and a little angry. What are her choices? (Invite another friend over; talk it over with her mother; etc.)

Singing Time Suggestions

"Choose the Right Way," 160

Conclusion

Reread the scripture together. Remind the children that Heavenly Father has helped them gain knowledge so that they can make choices that will make them happy and help them return to Heavenly Father's kingdom.

The Commandments

Purpose

To illustrate that the commandments offer us safety and protection.

Preparation

Prepare four road signs: Stop, Yield, Dead End, One Way.
Prepare five wordstrips: AND, KEEP, COMMANDMENTS, LIVE, MY.
Prepare display area, placing the wordstrips on one section and the road signs on another.

Application

Discussion: Display the four road signs. Focusing on one sign at a time, lead a discussion involving four areas: (1) Identify the sign. (2) Why is it used? (3) What should you do when you see it? (4) What would result if you disobeyed it?

Point out that all these signs are used to offer us protection. They warn us of dangers which may be ahead, and give caution for current conditions. Following these guidelines allows our journey to be much safer.

Next, liken these road signs to the commandments by pointing out that Heavenly Father has given us cautions and guidelines to keep our journey through earth life safe. These guidelines are known as the commandments.

Activity: Display the wordstrips. Explain that the words are mixed up and that they need to be put in the correct order to form a verse from the scriptures.

Guide the students in developing the following verse: "Keep my commandments and live" (Proverbs 7:2).

Choral Reading: Invite the entire group to read the completed verse out loud.

Discussion: Briefly discuss two or three of the commandments, using the same set of questions that were used for the road signs. Talk about the benefits of following the commandments versus the drawbacks of ignoring them. Discuss with the children the blessings of obedience.

Share your testimony that the commandments show Heavenly Father's love for us as he desires to protect us.

Singing Time Suggestions

"Keep the Commandments," 146

The Creation

Purpose

To help the children gain an understanding that the Creation displays Heavenly Father's great love for us.

Materials Needed

Seven pictures: the world (OQ196), light divided from darkness (OQ479), firmament (OQ480), Earth (OQ481), lights (OQ482), living creatures (OQ483), Adam and Eve (OQ461); chalkboard; chalk.

Preparation

Print the words of the following scriptures on individual slips of paper: Genesis 1:1, 1:3–4, 1:9, 1:11, 1:16, 1:24, 1:27.

Prepare a beautifully wrapped package.

Application

Game: Pass out the pictures and scripture slips to the children randomly. Invite the children with pictures to stand in front of the group. (Make sure the pictures are not in the correct order of the Creation.) Call on the children with scriptures to read their verse individually to the group. (Be sure the verses are in the proper order.) After the verse is read, have the group choose the picture which matches the verse. This continues until all the pictures are in order depicting the Creation.

Brainstorming: Begin this activity by having the children name their five senses: sight, hearing, touch, smell, and taste. List them in separate columns on the chalkboard. Challenge the children to think of all the wonderful things Heavenly Father created which satisfy our senses. (Example: a cool breeze satisfies the sense of touch.) Encourage the students to be creative by thinking of things which don't seem obvious. Allow them to brainstorm briefly. Write their ideas in the appropriate categories on the chalkboard.

Object Lesson: Display the decorative package. Explain that if we wanted to give someone a gift, we could put it in a plain box or bag. We could even hand it to them completely unwrapped. However, if we really wanted to show someone how much we loved them, we could carefully wrap it with beautiful paper and lavish it with lovely bows and other frills. Think about how special it is to receive a gift like that. It shows how much thought, time, and effort went into preparing and giving the gift.

Heavenly Father could have planned a place for us to live that was plain and without beauty. Because he loves us dearly, though, he desired to make the place where we were to live very special. He took great care to plan and prepare things which would bring pleasure to all of our senses. He used great detail and variety to please us.

Singing Time Suggestions

"God's Love," 97
"My Heavenly Father Loves Me," 228
"Because God Loves Me," 234

Conclusion

Challenge the children to continue to ponder the beauties and details of all that Heavenly Father has created for us. This is a means for us to always feel Heavenly Father's great love.

Dealing with Trials

Purpose

To help the children understand that dealing correctly with adversity will help them learn and become better members of the Church.

Materials Needed

Several pieces of sandpaper; several pieces of rough wood; several pieces of smooth, sanded wood.

Preparation

Print Doctrine and Covenants 98:12 on a lineboard. ("For he will give unto the faithful line upon line, precept upon precept; and I will try you and prove you herewith.")

Prepare to tell "Albert's Bike."

Application

Object Lesson: Have the children feel the sandpaper. Ask them how it feels. Pass a piece of rough wood and a piece of sanded wood around for the children to feel. Ask if they can feel a difference. Even though we would not like to wear sandpaper, it is very useful for smoothing rough wooden items. When the wood is smooth, we see the grain or the pattern of the wood better. All of the beautiful, finished wood we see has been smoothed and made beautiful with the help of sandpaper.

Tell the children that even though sandpaper does wonderful things for wood, if it is not used correctly it can be very damaging. It can leave scratches in the wood that can only be taken out with great effort; someone who uses sandpaper to make wood beautiful must use it the right way.

Liken the sandpaper to trials or times of trouble in our lives. Tell the children that all of us have trouble or things that do not go quite right.

11

When we learn from these trials, they help bring us closer to our Heavenly Father—we become more spiritually polished. If we are busy complaining, or if we begin to hate others or want to "get even" because of our trials, then we are using them the wrong way.

Choral Reading and Discussion: Read with the children the scripture on the lineboard.

In this scripture, what is the promise Heavenly Father makes if we do all that we should and we are proved faithful? (He will add to our knowledge.)

Why do you think that Heavenly Father allows us to experience trials in our lives? (To give us experience, to prove how much we love him, to help us see our blessings and be grateful, etc.)

How we act during our trials or troubles is very important. Heavenly Father wants us to show faith when we have trials. He knows that when we complain or become angry over our troubles we lose the Spirit. He also waits for us to ask his help because he loves us and wants to help us be closer to him.

Story: "Albert's Bike"

Albert's dad was decided. Albert would need to earn the money to fix his bike. It seemed so unfair—other people just got new bikes. Albert said a prayer inside his head. If only he could understand why it had to be this way.

Albert knew, though, that he would have to earn the money. Every Saturday he went to the Joneses' to mow their lawn, and every Wednesday evening he helped Mr. Evans with his new fence. Through the weeks, Albert carefully decided how best to spend his small amount of money. He paid his tithing and saved as much as he could, even sacrificing some activities. Finally, he had saved enough to fix his bike.

True to his word, Albert's dad took Albert to the store, carefully teaching him about cost and quality. With careful buying, Albert was able to get all that he needed to repair his bike.

The next evening, Albert and his dad took apart, cleaned, and repaired Albert's bike. Albert marveled that his dad knew so much about bikes.

"Learned the same way you have," Albert's dad said with a gentle laugh.

Discussion: What are some of the things that Albert learned from this experience? (How to work, how to save his money, good buying habits, how to fix a bike, etc.)

Do you think he will be able to use some of these things later in his life? How?

Was it harder to fix the bike than to replace it with a brand new one?

Which way would teach him more?

Could Albert have made this a bad experience? How?

Singing Time Suggestions

"Choose the Right Way," 160

Conclusion

Tell the children that even though trials are hard, we can learn from them. By staying close to Heavenly Father, even when things don't go right, we can learn from our troubles and mistakes and become closer to him.

Discernment

Purpose

To gain an understanding that Heavenly Father has given us the ability to discern good from evil.

Preparation

Prepare four activity centers using the following materials—

1. Four clear glass jars containing varying shades of blue water. Objective: To arrange water from the lightest shade to the darkest.
2. Several pairs of white socks, all different styles or sizes. Objective: To match all the socks.
3. Several soft items and several hard items. (Example: cotton balls, feather, scarf, rock, stick, marble.) Objective: To categorize soft items and hard items.
4. Four strips of poster board cut in varying lengths. Objective: To put the strips in order from shortest to longest.

Arrange to have someone to instruct in each activity center.

Print the entire verse of Moroni 7:15 on a lineboard. ("For behold, my brethren, it is given unto you to judge, that ye may know good from evil; and the way to judge is as plain, that ye may know with a perfect knowledge, as the daylight is from the dark night.")

Application

Activity Centers: Divide your students into small groups. Rotate the groups through each activity center.

Discussion: After each group has had a chance to complete the activity centers, begin your discussion. Which senses did the children use to help do the various activities? (Sight, touch, etc.) Point out how quickly and skillfully they were able to discern (or figure out) how each area worked.

During our earth life we are faced with many choices which require discernment to judge good from evil. Heavenly Father has given us spiritual abilities similar to our physical senses that help us distinguish good from evil just as we distinguished one object from another at the activity centers.

Choral Reading: Read the verse on your lineboard.

Activity: This activity will allow the children to practice discerning good from evil. Instruct them to listen carefully to the examples which are read. If it is good they should put their thumbs up. If it is evil their thumbs should point down.

1. Lisa always uses things that belong to others without asking.
2. David never forgets his morning or evening prayers.
3. Jessie watches dancing shows. The dancers wear clothes which are not modest.
4. April's parents tell her to be home by eight, but she comes home whenever she wants to.
5. Tracy never raises her voice at other people, even if she gets upset.
6. Wade pays his tithing each time he earns money.
7. Terry ignores his brothers and sisters when they need help.
8. Julie listens carefully when the family reads scriptures each day.
9. Thomas complains ever time Mother serves food he doesn't like.
10. Jay's friends wanted him to try a cigarette. He told them no.

Singing Time Suggestions

"Chose the Right Way," 160
"I Will Be Valiant," 162

Conclusion

Point out how easy it was for us to tell the right from the wrong today. Remind the children that Heavenly Father has given them that ability so that they might use it wisely and always make choices which will return them to their heavenly home.

Faith

Purpose

To help children understand what faith is and how we develop it.

Materials Needed

A chalkboard, chalk, eraser.

Preparation

Select prayerfully an individual to share a personal, faith-promoting story with your group. Explain the objective of your lesson to your guest.

Application

Discussion: Ask the following three questions of your group.

What would happen if you sat in one of the chairs in the room? (It would hold you up.)

What would happen if you turned the light switch off? (The lights would go out.)

What would happen if you pressed a piece of chalk against the chalkboard and moved it around? (It would write.)

Now try all three of the "experiments." Afterwards ask the children how they could know the results of the experiments before they happened.

They were able to know because they have experienced these things over and over again. They have begun to trust the results. Share an example. The first time a baby turns a light switch off and on, it surprises him. But as he does it again and again it doesn't surprise him anymore. He has developed faith in that light switch.

Brainstorming: Encourage the children to look around them and discover the everyday things they do by faith. Allow them to brainstorm ideas for a couple of minutes. Briefly review the many things they think of. Remind them that all these things are done in faith, and that faith was developed through experiencing these things many times.

Discussion: Help the students to understand that that is the way spiritual faith is developed also. Share another example. If you are sick, your father gives you a priesthood blessing. You begin to recover quickly.

At first this surprises you. As you grow up you receive more blessings when you need them. Gradually the results don't surprise you anymore. You have developed faith in the priesthood power. You know what the results will be before they happen.

Brainstorming: Heavenly Father desires to help us in our lives. He wants us to trust him with our needs. If we will go to him, he will answer our prayers each time. Gradually our faith in him will grow.

What things can we seek Heavenly Father's help with? Let the children brainstorm for a couple of minutes. Record all their thoughts on a chalkboard. Afterwards point out that all the ideas they came up with are opportunities to strengthen their faith.

Singing Time Suggestions

"I Pray in Faith," 14
"Faith," 96

Conclusion

Conclude by inviting the guest to share a personal experience which strengthened his or her faith.

Families

Purpose

To help students gain an understanding that Heavenly Father gives us families so that we may help and strengthen each other.

Materials Needed

Jewelry box, chalkboard, chalk, thermometer chart. (See the reusable visual section.)

Application

Object Lesson: Display the jewelry box. Point out the features. It is made of strong wood so that all the precious jewels can be kept in one safe place. It is lined with velvet so the jewels won't be scratched or damaged. There are separate compartments to keep the items from getting tangled together. These special boxes are designed to preserve and protect jewelry.

Remind the children that they are special jewels of Heavenly Father's. He loves them dearly and has created something wonderful to preserve and protect them during earth life. He created families.

Brainstorming: Begin by reading to your group the first of the three situations that follows. Give them three minutes to brainstorm ideas. Use one student to record the ideas on a chalkboard. Follow this same procedure for each situation. To encourage the children to participate and think of more ideas each time, use the thermometer chart. As the ideas increase, the temperature on the chart also increases.

1. Patricia is the youngest child in her family. She sometimes feels that no one likes her. What can her family do to help Patricia?
2. Daniel is having a hard time learning to read. What can his family do to help?
3. Mother is very sick. She has to stay in bed. What can the family do to help?

Praise the group for their creative thinking. Point out that this is why Heavenly Father put us together in families. We can help each other in many ways. We must watch carefully and always be thinking of special ways to help our family.

Game: There are some very important things which we should always be doing for the members of our family. The children will have to figure out what these things are by playing Hangman. Use the following words for your game: *pray, fast, gratitude,* and *example.* Briefly explain why each is important.

Singing Time Suggestions

"Love One Another," 136
"Home," 192

Conclusion

Challenge the group to always keep their eyes open for new ways to help their families.

Follow the Prophet

Purpose

To help the children understand that following the prophet will lead to happiness.

Materials Needed

Six pictures: Noah (OQ053), Isaiah (OQ339), Lehi (OQ517), Daniel (OQ531), Samuel the Lamanite (OQ370), current Church President.

Application

Activity: Have a child come to the front of the group and hold the first picture. Identify the prophet, talk about his picture, and proceed similarly with the other pictures.

1. Noah: Told the people to repent and live the commandments or Heavenly Father would punish them. (OQ053)
2. Isaiah: Saw the birth of the Savior. (OQ339)
3. Lehi: Preached to the people and told them to follow the commandments or Jerusalem would be destroyed. (OQ517)
4. Daniel: Interpreted Nebuchadnezzar's dream when no one else could. (OQ531)
5. Samuel the Lamanite: Foretold the birth of Christ to the Nephite people. (OQ370)

Tell the children that these prophets were very spiritual men. They loved the Savior and tried to help the people learn about him. Sometimes the people listened to what the prophet said and repented, and sometimes they did not. When a prophet said something would happen, it happened. Heavenly Father helped them know about future events. This is called revelation.

Discussion: What does a prophet do? (He receives messages from Heavenly Father.)

Who can be a prophet? (A man who has lived righteously, obeyed Heavenly Father's commandments, and holds the Melchizedek Priesthood.)

Why does Heavenly Father want us to have prophets? (Following the prophet will help us choose the right, will make us happy, will help us to follow the Savior, etc.)

Who is our prophet today? (Show the Church President's picture.) What has he asked us to do? (Read the Book of Mormon, obey our parents, etc.) Why would Heavenly Father want us to do these things? (Answers will vary.)

Tell the children that when we hear a prophet speak to us it's as though Heavenly Father is speaking to us. If we obey the words of a prophet, we will find happiness in all that we do and we will be able to follow Jesus.

Singing Time Suggestions

"Follow the Prophet," 110 (especially last verse)
"Stand for the Right," 159

Conclusion

Hold up the President's picture and tell the children that if we follow the teachings of the prophet we will find real happiness.

Following Jesus

Purpose

To help the children understand what following Jesus means.

Materials Needed

Display area; six pictures: Jesus the Christ (OQ572), John baptizing Jesus (OQ133), Jesus praying with Nephites (OQ542), boy Jesus in the temple (OQ500), Christ and the children (OQ467), Jesus healing Nephites (OQ541); chalkboard; chalk.

Preparation

Cut six sets of adult footprints from paper.

Print the first part of John 12:26 on a lineboard. ("If any man serve me, let him follow me.")

Prepare slips of paper with one of the following words on each: *baptism, prayer, scriptures, service, love.*

Prepare display area by placing picture OQ572 at the center. The lineboard should be set up next to the picture.

Arrange the footprints so they are leading to the Savior's picture in the display area.

Application

Choral Reading and Discussion: Read together the scripture on the lineboard.

Who said this? (Jesus)

Why does Jesus want us to follow him? (So that he can lead us back to Heavenly Father.)

Tell the children that following in the footsteps of Jesus will help them to become closer to Heavenly Father.

Activity: Have a child stand on the set of footprints farthest from the display area. Tell the children that Jesus has left a path for us to follow. When we do what Jesus has done and follow his path, we can come closer to him.

Have a child select one of the pieces of paper. Read the topic and explain how Jesus accomplished that topic. Post the picture on the display area, or a child may do this. As each topic is discussed the child on the footprints will advance one set toward the display area.

1. Baptism: Jesus was baptized by John the Baptist. He knew that he had to be baptized so that he could live with Heavenly Father again. (OQ133)
2. Prayer: Jesus often prayed to Heavenly Father to help him when he was sad, when he needed Heavenly Father's inspiration, or when he was grateful. (OQ542)
3. Scriptures: Jesus studied the scriptures when he was a child and when he grew up. This is the reason he knew the scriptures so well and was able to understand Heavenly Father so well. (OQ500)
4. Love: Jesus loved everyone around him, even when they hurt him. He tried to show his love all the time. He especially loved children. (OQ467)
5. Service: Jesus always helped other people. Sometimes he helped by listening, and other times he helped by using his priesthood. (OQ541)

Discussion: What are some things you can do to show Jesus that you are following him? (Keep the commandments, be baptized, be a missionary, help others, be kind, read or listen to the scriptures, pray, etc.) You may want to use a chalkboard to list the answers. If times permits, talk about the answers.

Singing Time Suggestions

"I'm Trying to Be like Jesus," 78
"Come, Follow Me," *Hymns*, no. 116

Conclusion

Have the children read the lineboard scripture out loud. Remind them that following Jesus will help us return to Heavenly Father. Challenge them to try harder to walk in Jesus' footprints.

Following the Prophets

Purpose

To help the children gain an understanding of what it means to follow the prophets.

Materials Needed

Picture of Ezra Taft Benson (OQ576), chalkboard, chalk, eraser.

Preparation

Prepare to tell "Brandon's Lamb."

Read President Benson's pamphlet *To the Children of the Church*. Mark any section from the pamphlet which you feel is especially applicable to your students.

Application

Chalkboard Story: "Brandon's Lamb" (Have a child draw parts of this story on the chalkboard as you tell it.)

There once was a young boy named Brandon. He lived on a farm. (Draw a boy.) One warm summer day his father asked him if he would like a lamb of his very own. Brandon was very excited, and he promised to take good care of the lamb.

Father went to buy Brandon's lamb. While he was gone, Brandon began to get the barn ready. (Draw a barn.) First he filled the pen with sweet-smelling straw. This would make a soft bed for his lamb. (Draw the straw.) Next he carried buckets and buckets of cool, clean water and poured them in a big, metal tub for the lamb to drink from. (Draw a bucket of water.) Then Brandon took two big scoops of oats from a barrel and put them in a feed box. Now his lamb would have plenty to eat. (Draw a box.)

Brandon waited a long time until he finally saw his father coming in the truck. (Draw a truck.) Father stopped the truck next to Brandon, and together they unloaded his lamb. (Draw a lamb.)

Brandon's father handed him the rope. He told Brandon to take good care of the lamb and to lead him to the barn. Then Brandon's father went into the house. Brandon rubbed the lamb's wooly back and scratched its ears.

Then he took up the lead rope and began to lead the lamb to the barn. A funny thing happened. The lamb sat down in the dirt and refused to move. Brandon pulled on the rope, but the lamb refused to budge. He tried pushing and gently coaxing it, but it still sat in the dirt.

Brandon tried to explain that in the barn was fresh food, water, and a comfortable place to sleep. The little lamb didn't understand. He stubbornly sat in the dirt on a hot, summer day instead of walking to the barn that had been prepared especially for him and where he would be comfortable and happy.

Discussion: Write the word *heaven* above the picture of the barn. Explain that Heavenly Father has prepared wonderful things for us in heaven. Write the word *prophet* above the drawing of the little boy. Heavenly Father has appointed a prophet to lead our church. Our prophet wants to lead us back to our heavenly home. He does this through sharing revelations and giving us counsel. Write the word *us* above the lamb. If we refuse to follow the prophet by not doing what he says, then we are like the lamb sitting in the dirt on a hot, summer day. We are led by the prophet only when we are obedient to his words.

Activity: Read a previously selected section from President Benson's pamphlet to the children. Have the children raise their hands each time they hear something which the prophet has instructed them to do. Instruct one child to make a tally mark on the chalkboard each time the group raises their hands. Afterwards count up the tally marks. Challenge the group to see if they can recall each of the instructions they have heard. (Example: if there were eight tally marks, they should be able to remember eight items of instruction.)

Singing Time Suggestions

"Seek the Lord Early," 108
"Latter-day Prophets," 134

Conclusion

Conclude by bearing your testimony that following the prophet will lead us to eternal life.

Following the Savior

Purpose

To help the children understand that following the Savior can make their lives happy.

Materials Needed

Length of yarn, plastic bag with several large beads of various colors, pattern instructions (type your own), picture of the Savior (OQ572), chalkboard, chalk.

Application

Object Lesson: Show the bag of beads to the children. Tell them that you have seen a beautiful pattern in these colors and, if you are very careful, you can string these beads to make the same pleasing pattern. As you begin to string the beads, tell the children that you must always keep the pattern in mind so that you will know which bead to use next. Sometimes, you may forget where you are on the pattern and when that happens you need to look at the instructions again to remember how it looks. (Show the instructions.)

Show the finished pattern to the children and let them know how glad you are that it looks so good.

Hold up a picture of the Savior. Tell the children how much you love and appreciate the Savior and the life he lived. Explain that the pattern, or example, he set is the one you want to follow. Tell them that Jesus showed us the best pattern for living. If we are careful and always remember to follow Jesus, we will continue to see a pleasing pattern in our lives. Remind them that prayer and scriptures are like instructions. (Hold up the scriptures.) They can help us remember the pattern we want in our lives.

Chalkboard Discussion: Ask if anyone can tell you some things that will help us have a pleasing pattern in our lives. (Helping other people, being kind, keeping the commandments, etc.) List them on the chalkboard as the children think of them.

Singing Time Suggestions

"He Sent His Son," 34

Conclusion

Show the picture of the Savior and remind the children how they will feel if they follow the pattern shown by the Savior.

Friendship

Purpose

To help the children understand that our friendships are affected by how we treat other people.

Materials Needed

One large heart, two silhouettes of girls, two silhouettes of boys, thumbtacks, string, display area.

Preparation

Print the first part of Proverbs 17:17 on the heart. ("A friend loveth at all times.")

Prepare the display area by putting the heart in the middle. Place a pair of silhouettes on each side of the heart. Using thumbtacks, tack a string leading from each silhouette to the heart. Although the silhouettes may be either taped or tacked in place, the heart should be held by thumbtacks only.

Application

Activity: Draw attention to the display area. Point out that friendship is a special feeling that is shared with other people. Special feelings must be tended carefully or they may be lost. Relate the following examples of what can happen.

1. Susan and Anna are playing together. Anna starts to make fun of Susan. Soon names are called back and forth and a friendship is broken. (Untack one of the bottom strings from the heart.)
2. Jimmy pushed Aaron because he wanted to be first. The first push led to another, and soon Aaron and Jimmy were hitting and hurting each other. Another friendship is broken. (Untack the other bottom string from the heart.)

3. Milly had a bag of candy but wouldn't share with Justin at all. After a big argument over sharing and selfishness, Justin went home. Is their friendship hurt? (Untack one of the top strings to the heart.)

At this point the heart is held by one thumbtack. Tell the children that when we do or say unkind things, when we think only of ourselves, when we make fun of others or call them names, we can hurt our friendships with other people.

Discussion: What can we do to strengthen our friendships? (Share, help each other, try to understand, be thoughtful, etc.)

With each positive answer tack the strings back to the heart until the heart is secure again. (Use extra strings and thumbtacks if necessary.)

Read with the children the scripture on the heart. Remind them that how we act towards others shows them how we feel about them. Being a good friend is not a magical trick but an accomplishment that takes work and love.

Singing Time Suggestions

"Friends Are Fun," 262
"A Prayer," 22

Conclusion

Remind the children that friendship is a valuable gift and should be treasured and treated carefully. Have them read the scripture (Proverbs 17:17) with you.

29

Gifts of the Spirit

Purpose

To help the children understand that every spiritual gift comes from Jesus through the Spirit.

Preparation

Prepare eight pictures of gift boxes. On the back of each picture put the name of one spiritual gift: wisdom, knowledge, faith, gift of healing, working of miracles, prophecy, discernment, gift of tongues.

Print the last part of Doctrine and Covenants 46:8 on one side of a lineboard. ("Seek ye earnestly the best gifts, always remembering for what they are given.")

Application

Discussion: Tell the children that when we give a friend or family member a gift we want it to be nice. Remind them that we look and look until we find just the right gift for our friends or family because we love them.

What are some gifts we would give to a friend or a member of our family?

Explain that Heavenly Father gives us many gifts because he loves us. We can see his gifts all around us. Tell the children some of the gifts that you can see.

Have the children read the lineboard scripture with you.

What kinds of gifts do you think Heavenly Father wants us to seek?

Activity: Ask the children if they think the gifts Heavenly Father wants us to seek are the best TVs or cars or homes. Explain that when Heavenly Father talks about the best gifts, he's talking about eternal gifts, or spiritual gifts. The scriptures tell us about these gifts and call them gifts of the Spirit.

Tell the children that if we turn these pictures over, we will find what some of these gifts are. Have a child come and choose one of the pictures. Turn the picture over and read the name of the gift. Explain what that gift of the Spirit is. Repeat until each gift is named.

Remind the children that Heavenly Father has many spiritual gifts waiting for us, but we must seek them and work to deserve them. Tell the group that he wants us to receive the gift of the Spirit that will be best for us. Explain the difference between these gifts and others—when we receive them we must share them and use them to help other people. When we do this it will make our gift even better and bring us closer to Heavenly Father.

Singing Time Suggestions

"The Still Small Voice," 106

Conclusion

Some of the best gifts that Heavenly Father has given us are gifts of the Spirit. These are very special gifts that can help us return to him. If we try to keep the commandments and do what Jesus wants us to, we can receive a gift of the Spirit too.

Gratitude

Purpose

To teach children that expressing gratitude is an important part of prayer.

Materials Needed

Bean bag.

Preparation

Prepare to tell "Staci's Garden."

Read Luke 17:11–19 and be prepared to tell the story of the ten lepers in your own words.

Print the entire verse of 1 Thessalonians 5:18 on a lineboard. ("In every thing give thanks: for this is the will of God in Christ Jesus concerning you.")

Print the phrase "Gratitude Attitude" on the opposite side of the lineboard.

Application

Story: "Staci's Garden"

Staci was eight years old. Her older brother Jeff was going to be twelve years old on his next birthday, and that was only eight weeks away. Staci loved Jeff and wanted to give him a very special present. She knew just what he wanted. He had been asking for a watch for a long time. Staci looked in the store and found that watches were very expensive.

She talked with her father about it. He suggested that Staci take care of their garden to earn extra money for Jeff's gift. Staci worked hard each day in the garden. She pulled the weeds and watered the vegetables. The raspberries began to ripen, so she picked them and put them in little plastic baskets. Sometimes the thorns from the raspberry bushes would prick her fingers. Other times she would get hot in the warm summer sunshine. But whenever she got discouraged she just thought about how happy Jeff would be to get his new watch.

Two days before Jeff's birthday Staci had finally earned enough money for the watch. Mother took her to the store. Staci picked out the watch and proudly paid for it. When she got home she wrapped it in bright yellow paper and put a big bow on top.

Finally the special day came. Jeff opened presents while everyone ate birthday cake. Staci hoped he would choose hers first, and he did! She watched anxiously as he tore off the yellow paper. He admired the watch and carefully strapped it on his wrist.

Staci kept waiting for Jeff to say something to her. But he didn't. Jeff didn't even say thank you.

How do you think Staci felt?

Do you think she would want to work as hard next year to buy Jeff a gift?

Why not?

Discussion: Point out the importance of saying thank you to others. It is a way of showing gratitude. It shows appreciation for special things which are given to or done for us.

Scripture Story: Explain that there are many stories in the scriptures which teach us about showing gratitude. Invite ten class members to come up in front of your group. In your own words, tell the story of the ten lepers. Separate one child from the group of ten to illustrate how many forgot to thank Jesus.

How do you think Jesus felt?

Do we ever forget to thank Heavenly Father?

Game: Toss a bean bag to class members. When they catch it they must name a blessing they're thankful for. Try to give everyone a chance to participate.

Discussion: Use the bean bag game to illustrate how many wonderful things they have been given. Explain to them the importance of remembering to thank Heavenly Father in all of our prayers. Expressing our gratitude is so important that we are taught that after we address Heavenly Father in prayer, giving thanks is the very first thing we should do.

Choral Reading: As a group, read the verse printed on the lineboard.

Singing Time Suggestions

"I Thank Thee, Dear Father," 7
"Can a Little Child like Me?" 9

Conclusion

To help them remember this concept, turn the lineboard over to display the phrase "Gratitude Attitude." Have the group repeat it with you. Encourage the children to always have a "gratitude attitude" by remembering to thank Heavenly Father each time they pray.

Gratitude for Blessings

Purpose

To help the children understand and talk about gratitude.

Materials Needed

Display area.

Preparation

Cut sixteen four-by-four-inch squares of poster board. Using pictures or simple drawings, prepare two copies of each drawing you choose. You might draw a temple, a family, a happy face, a sad face, the Book of Mormon, fresh foods, a prophet, or musical notes. Words may be used instead of pictures but are not the best option.

Arrange the game by mixing the pairs up and placing them face down on the display area.

Application

Game: Tell the children that today you will be playing a matching game. Allow a child the choice of two squares. Turn those two squares over. If the squares do not match, return the squares to their face-down position and repeat. When a match is made, remove the squares and ask a "thought question." Repeat until all the squares have been matched or time is gone.

Examples of "thought questions":

1. Temple: Why does Heavenly Father want us to have temples?
2. Family: Why did Heavenly Father give us families?
3. Happy Face: Name something that makes you happy.
4. Sad Face: What is something you can do to make you happy when you're sad?
5. Book of Mormon: Why is reading the Book of Mormon a good thing for us to do?

6. Fresh Foods: What kind of fruit (or vegetable) do you like best?
7. Prophet: Why did Heavenly Father give us a prophet?
8. Musical Notes: What is your favorite song?

Explain to the children that these are just a few of the blessings that Heavenly Father has given us. Tell them that if they think about it, they will find many, many blessings that Heavenly Father has given them.

Singing Time Suggestions

"I Am Glad for Many Things," 151
"Can a Little Child like Me?" 9

Conclusion

Remind the children to think about their own personal blessings. If you have time, bear your testimony.

Grudges

Purpose

To help the children understand that holding a grudge keeps us from being happy.

Materials Needed

Five or six wads of newspaper, small garbage sack.

Preparation

Print the first part of Ephesians 4:32 on a lineboard. ("And be ye kind one to another, tenderhearted, forgiving one another.")
Prepare to tell "Joyce's Story I" and "Joyce's Story II."

Application

Discussion: Ask the children what a grudge is. (Being unable to forget something someone did or said that made you feel bad.) Holding a grudge is like holding some garbage; if you carry it too long, you will start to smell like the garbage too.

Activity and Story: Tell the children that you would like their help getting the "garbage thoughts" or grudges out of this story. Have one child hold the garbage sack and another the wads of newspaper. Have them help you by putting a wad of newspaper into the garbage when something in the story shows that Joyce holds a grudge. (These instances are indicated by "G.T.")

"Joyce's Story I"

Joyce was mad! Megan, her best friend, had said some pretty mean things to her last week. Mother had tried to remind Joyce that she had said some pretty mean things too, but Joyce's feelings were really hurt and now she couldn't think of Megan without feeling angry. (G.T.)

Today was a Saturday. The sun was shining brightly outside. Make the bed, clean the room, straighten the books, vacuum the floor, and practice the piano—these were Joyce's chores today. Practicing the piano, especially the scales, reminded Joyce that Megan was learning to play the piano too.

"How did I ever choose her to be my friend?" Joyce thought. "She's such a mean person." (G.T.)

Usually, after her chores were done, Joyce would go over to Megan's house to play.

"Not ever again," thought Joyce out loud. "Not after those terrible things she said." (G.T.)

Instead, Joyce walked to the mall with her big sister, Kate. Kate was looking for a new dress and found a blue one with white lace that she liked.

Joyce took one look at that dress and thought, "That's the color that Megan likes. The more I think about what she said, the worse it sounds." (G.T.)

After shopping, Kate took Joyce to get an ice cream. The store was cool after walking in the hot, afternoon sun. Joyce was careful not to choose a kind of ice cream that Megan liked.

"Megan always chooses such strange flavors! I'll bet she really wanted me to feel bad and said everything on purpose." (G.T.)

As they continued the walk home Kate tried to talk to Joyce but soon gave up because Joyce just wasn't talking. The sisters walked into the house to find Mother cooking dinner.

"How was your day, Joyce?" Mother asked.

Joyce sat down hard on a kitchen chair and said, "What a terrible Saturday! Nothing good happened."

Ask the children what Joyce's day may have been like if she hadn't been holding a grudge.

"Joyce's Story II"

Today was a Saturday. The sun was shining brightly outside. Make the bed, clean the room, straighten the books, vacuum the floor, and practice the piano—these were Joyce's chores today. Practicing the piano, especially the scales, was hard, but Joyce knew that if she practiced, it would get easier.

She looked out of the window and saw the gentle breeze swaying the trees. The sun warmed the air and made Joyce look forward to being outside.

Usually, as soon as her chores were done, Joyce would go over to Megan's house to play. But today Kate, her big sister, invited her to go for a walk to the mall.

Kate was looking for a new dress and found a blue one with white lace. Joyce did some looking also and found a pretty dress in pink. She would have to drop a hint to her mom. After all, her birthday was just a couple of months away.

After shopping, Kate and Joyce stopped to get an ice cream. The store was cool after walking in the hot, afternoon sun. Even though Joyce usually got Strawberry Deluge, today would be different and she would try the newest flavor, EverBerry.

As they finished the walk home Kate and Joyce talked about many things: Kate's classes at high school; Joyce's new teacher; the heat; and their little brother, Ted. Before they knew it they were home and walked in to find Mother cooking dinner.

"How was your day, Joyce?" Mother asked.

"Oh, Mom," she said, "we did so many fun things."

Discussion: Ask the children if there was a difference in Joyce's day. Why? How do Jesus and Heavenly Father feel about grudges? (They want us to get rid of them.) Why? (Because if we're feeling angry or mad we can't listen to the Holy Ghost, we should never judge another person.) How can we get rid of grudges? (Try not to think of them, replace them with other thoughts, pray to forgive another, etc.)

Tell the children that when we get rid of our bad feelings about another person, we are doing what the scriptures tell us we should.

Scripture Reading: Display lineboard and have children read Ephesians 4:32 with you.

Singing Time Suggestions

"Help Me, Dear Father," 99

Conclusion

Remind the children that when we are able to get rid of our bad thoughts we can be happier. Reread the scripture and, if time permits, bear your own personal testimony about this principle.

Holy Ghost

Purpose

To illustrate how the Holy Ghost gives us direction in our lives and to encourage the students to listen carefully for the still, small voice.

Preparation

Cut a string nine feet long. Affix it vertically to a wall where the children can see it.

Select a picture of a field of corn from a book or encyclopedia.

Print on several small papers sample situations which would require guidance from the Holy Ghost. (Example: Bobby earned fifty dollars during the summer. What should he do with it?) Fold the papers and put them in a hat.

Prepare to tell "Rachelle and the Cornfield."

Application

Discussion: Begin your lesson by showing the picture of a cornfield to your group. Show them the string and explain that a corn stalk is about nine feet tall. Invite a few children to stand next to the string to compare the size difference. It is so tall that we would never be able to see over it. Tell them that corn in a field grows so close together that it is impossible to see through it. Share the following story.

Story: "Rachelle and the Cornfield"

Entering the cornfield was like a whole new world for five-year-old Rachelle. Tall, green stalks waved high above her, and broad, flat leaves slithered along her neck and tickled at her nose. What fun it was running through the maze of corn rows and pretending to hide! No one could find her in this cornfield, she giggled to herself. Not even Mommy or Daddy.

Thinking of Mommy and Daddy made her realize how hot and itchy it was in the cornfield. Time to go home, she decided. She followed a row of corn in the direction she thought was home. After walking for a couple of minutes, she began to feel unsure. If only she could see her house. But

40

nothing could be seen over the tall stalks of corn. She tried standing on tiptoes and even jumping, but still not a glimpse of home.

Starting to feel a little frightened, Rachelle began to run. First this way, then that way, desperately trying to find her way back to safety. As she ran she started to cry and call for Mommy and Daddy. She ran until she was out of breath and her legs were shaking. Sinking down to the damp earth she sobbed with fear. She was lost in this big field and couldn't find her way out.

Suddenly, she thought she heard something. She tried to quit crying so she could hear better.

She could hear a voice calling to her from a great distance. She got up and slowly walked towards the sound of the voice. She stopped to listen from time to time, as even the slight sounds of her walking would drown out the voice.

As Rachelle drew closer, the voice became clearer. She recognized it as Daddy calling her name. Rachelle began to quicken her pace. Daddy kept talking to her, instructing her to keep following his voice. He reassured her and told her he loved her.

His voice was louder and clearer and Rachelle could tell she was very near the edge of the cornfield. A cool breeze and the bright light of the day burst upon Rachelle as she came through the last row of corn. The look of concern left Mommy's and Daddy's faces as she returned to their loving arms.

Discussion: Help the group to understand the meaning of the story by asking the following questions.

Why was Rachelle frightened?

What did she hear that helped her?

What was the voice like?

Where did the voice lead her?

Explain that we had to leave our heavenly home when we came to earth. There will be times when each of us feels lost. We may not know which way to go. Heavenly Father is concerned and wants us to find our way home. To help us, he has given us the Holy Ghost. The Holy Ghost is a small, quiet voice. To hear the Holy Ghost, we have to stop and listen very carefully, just as Rachelle had to listen closely to hear her father. The voice will give us directions that we must follow if we want to find our way home. The Holy Ghost will also comfort us so the journey back will not be so frightening.

Buzz Session: Divide your students into small groups. Allow each group to choose a prepared paper from the hat. Instruct them to quietly read the situation to their group and then have a brief buzz session to decide what the

Holy Ghost would say to us in that situation. After a few minutes, have each group report on their situation and the ideas they thought of.

Singing Time Suggestions

"The Holy Ghost," 105
"The Still Small Voice," 106
"Listen, Listen," 107

Conclusion

Briefly conclude by asking the children to watch for situations in their own lives similar to those discussed in the buzz session. Encourage them to listen carefully for those quiet promptings.

Individual Worth

Purpose

To help each child feel his worth as a child of God.

Materials Needed

Magnifying mirror, ordinary mirror, popsicle stick for each child, a container for storage of the popsicle sticks, several marking pens.

Preparation

Arrange for each child to cut out a snowflake the week prior to your lesson. (This could possibly be done during individual class time if used in a Primary setting.)

Display the snowflakes all around the room.

Print Isaiah 13:12 on a lineboard. ("I will make a man more precious than fine gold.")

Application

Discussion: Snowflakes are wonderful. Each is beautiful and yet each is different. (Have the children look around the room.) Every snowflake was made from the same color and size of paper, but they still turned out differently.

Just as these snowflakes are beautiful but different, so are each of us. As children of Heavenly Father we are very important and precious. We are also different from each other. We have different thoughts, ideas, talents, and needs. We can all be different and also all be important.

Object Lesson: Pass both mirrors around for the children to view themselves. Explain that the magnifying mirror gives a distorted image of ourselves. If we thought we really looked like that we would become very discouraged. The ordinary mirror reflects the true image. We can use this mirror to make corrections in our appearance, helping us to feel comfortable with the way we look.

Liken the magnifying mirror to the distorted view society can give us about ourselves. If we relied on other people's opinions about us we would become discouraged. People can be critical, negative, and even untruthful in their judgments of us.

Heavenly Father offers us the true reflection of ourselves. He can clearly point out our strong points and talents. He also can gently show us those areas which need some adjustment. Through his accurate assessment we are able to reach our full potential. Heavenly Father's image of us builds our self-esteem and encourages us.

Activity: Give each child a popsicle stick. Hand out markers and instruct the children to write their names on the popsicle sticks. As they are doing this, explain to the group that each stick will be placed in a container. Children will be selected to answer questions or help the leaders as each popsicle stick is drawn from the container. Make sure the children understand that everyone must place their popsicle stick in the container because everyone is important and their help and opinions are valuable. (This container of labeled popsicle sticks will enable you to make sure that each child gets an opportunity to participate in future activities.) Tell the children that the container will be carefully stored and used frequently in Primary.

Singing Time Suggestions

"Every Star Is Different," 142
"Shine On," 144

Conclusion

Read the verse on your lineboard together. Help the children understand that they are very special in Heavenly Father's sight. His opinion of them is the one to value.

Latter-day Prophets

Purpose

To acquaint and familiarize the children with latter-day prophets.

Materials Needed

Pictures of each latter-day prophet (OQ449 to OQ460, OQ576).

Preparation

Prepare two wordstrips: PROPHET and LATTER-DAY.

Application

Discussion: Put up the wordstrip PROPHET. What does a prophet do? (Guides and directs the Church through revelation.) Now put the wordstrip LATTER-DAY in front of PROPHET and ask what that word means. (The time after the gospel was restored.) Tell the children that a LATTER-DAY PROPHET is one who guides and directs the restored Church.

Activity: Show the pictures and explain that these are pictures of prophets.

Give the children a few facts about the first latter-day prophet. Who was our first latter-day prophet? (Joseph Smith.) Have a child choose the picture of Joseph Smith and stand at the front of the class holding it.

Tell the class about Brigham Young. Who was this latter-day prophet? (Brigham Young.) Have a child stand next to the first child with his picture.

Continue until each of the prophets has been named and identified.

Use the following for your facts about the prophets, or use your own supplemental material.

1. Joseph Smith: His favorite sport was wrestling. He also played ball and liked to slide on the ice.
2. Brigham Young: When he was a young boy, he would get up in the middle of the night for a snack of bread and butter.
3. John Taylor: When he was a boy, he had a dream of an angel holding a trumpet, sending out a message to the world.
4. Wilford Woodruff: As a boy, he was one of the most successful fishermen in his village.
5. Lorenzo Snow: He was always very orderly and precise in everything he did. He was known for being very honest.
6. Joseph F. Smith: His family was so poor that until he was six, the main food they had was milk.
7. Heber J. Grant: When this prophet was a boy he would play marbles every spring, and usually won.
8. George Albert Smith: He loved being outdoors and especially liked swimming in the Jordan River.
9. David O. McKay: While growing up he had a dog, a pony, pigeons, rabbits, and a tame magpie.
10. Joseph Fielding Smith: He had a horse named Junie that could always get out of the barn no matter what he did to stop her.
11. Harold B. Lee: When he was a young boy he cut his long, curly hair so that other children wouldn't make fun of him.
12. Spencer W. Kimball: While milking the cow he memorized the Ten Commandments to the beat of milk squirting into the bucket.
13. Ezra Taft Benson: He was named after his great-grandfather who was in the Mormon Battalion. As a boy he enjoyed basketball, ice skating, and singing.

Singing Time Suggestions

"Latter-day Prophets," 134

Conclusion

Briefly go over the list of latter-day prophets in order. Remind the children that the more we learn about the prophets, the more we will appreciate them.

Looking for the Good

Purpose

To help children understand that everyone has good characteristics.

Materials Needed

Chalkboard, chalk.

Preparation

Prepare a wordstrip: CHARACTERISTIC.
Prepare a tray with several ordinary items on it: a paper clip, a rubber band, a safety pin, a needle, a light bulb, etc.

Application

Activity: Post the wordstrip CHARACTERISTIC and tell the children that it means something that describes what a person or thing does.

Show the children the objects you have on the tray. Tell them that although we may think of some of these things as ordinary, each one has at least one good characteristic. Discuss with the children the positive or good characteristics of each item.

Explain that every person has many good characteristics. When we see the good in people it makes us feel friendly and happy.

Discussion: As the children respond to the following questions, write their answers on the chalkboard.

Why should we look for the good in other people? (It's what Jesus did, we can make friends, etc.)

What must you do to find the good characteristics in every person? (Get to know them, don't judge, look for the good, etc.)

What are some good characteristics that we can look for in people? (Friendly, happy, thrifty, etc.)

Singing Time Suggestions

"Every Star Is Different," 142
"I'll Walk with You," 140
"Love One Another," 136

Conclusion

Challenge the children to try looking for the good in everyone they meet.

Missionary Work

Purpose

To illustrate that everyone needs to be a missionary, and to teach children what they can do to be missionaries now.

Materials Needed

Pencils for group, transparency marker, picture: calling of the fishermen (OQ496).

Preparation

Cut out enough paper dolls for your entire class. Affix dolls to a large surface and display for all to see.

Prepare to read Matthew 4:18–20.

Print the last part of Matthew 5:44 on a lineboard. ("Love your enemies, bless them that curse you, do good to them that hate you, and pray for them which despitefully use you, and persecute you.")

Application

Discussion: Show your group the paper cutouts. Explain that they represent all the children in your class. Invite the children to come forward a few at a time and take a paper doll for themselves. After they're seated, point out all the dolls that are left. They represent the children who are not at Primary. For various reasons, they were not able to come. Some of them may not understand the importance of coming to church. They are not able to listen to the music or hear the lessons. These children may not have anyone to teach them about the gospel. Express to the students the sorrow that Heavenly Father must feel because of this.

Scripture Story: Display the picture of Christ calling Peter and Andrew to follow him. Read Matthew 4:18–20 to the children. Christ wanted everyone to have the gospel. He needed help to teach the gospel to everyone, so he began to call people to help him. Explain that "fishers of men" means missionaries. He taught these men what they should do to be good missionaries.

Activity: Display your lineboard. Read the scripture aloud to them. Explain that in this verse, Jesus taught us the things we need to do for those who don't have the gospel.

What is the very first thing that he told his followers to do? (Love.) Let a child underline "love" on the lineboard. Direct the others to write "love" on their paper cutouts.

What are the second and third things he taught them to do? (Bless and do good.) Have another child come up and underline those words. Explain that to bless and do good means to serve. Have the children write "serve" on their paper cutouts.

What was the fourth thing he taught those who followed him to do? (Pray.) Have a child underline pray on the lineboard. Direct the others to write "pray" on their cutouts.

Go back to the board with the leftover cutouts on it. Help them understand that some of these children need to learn more about the gospel. We are the ones who Heavenly Father and Jesus need to help them. Jesus has asked us to follow him. Jesus was a wonderful missionary. If we want to follow him we must be missionaries too. He has already taught us how. The students can use their cutouts to remind them what they must do to be good missionaries.

Singing Time Suggestions

"I Want to Be a Missionary Now," 168
"The Things I Do," 170
"We'll Bring the World His Truth," 172

Conclusion

Review the three things the children can do to be missionaries. You can briefly talk about each to help them see how it applies to their lives.

Music

Purpose

To help the children understand that the music they sing was written to help them understand the gospel.

Preparation

Print the following names on a chalkboard: Mildred Pettit, Vanja Watkins, Merrill Bradshaw, Michael Moody, Joseph Ballantyne, Janice Kapp Perry.

Coordinate with others as needed in choosing and preparing to sing several songs from the *Children's Songbook*.

Prepare a large posterboard or paper star for each song and print a song's name on each board or star.

Print "Music can light my life" on a lineboard.

Application

Discussion: Tell the children that each of the people listed on the board wrote the words of at least one song in the *Children's Songbook*.

Explain that each of these people (point to the chalkboard) loves the gospel and wanted to share some of their feelings through music. In a very special way they used music to bear their testimony.

When we sing their songs, what would they want us to do? (Learn the words and listen to the music, try to understand what they want us to know.)

Activity: Have a child pick one of the stars. The chorister can then lead the children in singing that song (example: "I Am a Child of God"). After the song has been sung, ask the children what the composer (Sister Randall) wanted them to know. (That they are special because each is a child of God, that if they do what they should they can live with Heavenly Father.) As the children interpret the music place the star on the lineboard. Repeat this process, placing stars around the lineboard, as time permits.

51

Conclusion

Remind the children that when they try to understand what they sing about, they can bring special blessings into their lives.

Obedience Brings Blessings

Purpose

To show some of the blessings obedience brings.

Preparation

Print on a lineboard the first part of Doctrine and Covenants 130:21. ("And when we obtain any blessings from God, it is by obedience to that law.")

Select a child or a teacher to tell about a time they were obedient and the blessing they received because they were obedient.

Prepare the chalkboard by listing commandments (tithing, Sabbath day, Word of Wisdom, fasting, baptism, Book of Mormon, and the sacrament) on the right side and posting the lineboard at the top of the left side.

Application

Choral Reading and Discussion: Read the scripture on the lineboard with the children.

What does this scripture tell us? (That when we obey a commandment, we will receive a blessing.)

Tell the children that Heavenly Father has made promises through the scriptures and his prophets that if we are obedient and obey his commandments he will bless us.

Activity: Point to the list of commandments on the chalkboard. Tell the children that you will read a blessing and they must choose the commandment that best goes with it. As a commandment is chosen, erase it from the list and rewrite it under the lineboard.

1. Tithing: Windows of heaven are opened and blessings are poured out.
2. Sabbath Day: Helps us feel spiritually new as we remember the Savior and his sacrifice for us.

3. Word of Wisdom: Gives us good eating rules and can help us have a healthier body.
4. Fasting: Helps us become more humble and receptive to the Spirit.
5. Baptism: Takes away our sins. This is necessary for all people to have done before they can become members in Christ's church.
6. Book of Mormon: President Benson said that reading this brings peace to our lives.
7. The Sacrament: Helps us remember our baptismal covenants. When we do this, we should think about how much Jesus loves us.

Tell the children that Heavenly Father is a generous giver. He wants to give us blessings. He wants us to be the best we can be because he loves us.

Sharing Activity: Have a child or a teacher share their special experience with you and the children.

Singing Time Suggestions

"Keep the Commandments," 146

Conclusion

Reread the scripture on the lineboard. Tell the children that obedience not only brings blessings but makes us happy because we are doing what Heavenly Father wants us to do.

Obedience—Its Importance

Purpose

To help the children understand the importance of obedience.

Materials Needed

2 x 4 length of wood.

Preparation

Print part of Hebrews 13:17 on the lineboard. ("Obey them that have the rule over you, . . . for they watch for your souls.")
Prepare to tell "The Hike to Angle Canyon."

Application

Activity: Ask a child to walk on the floor beside the 2 x 4. Now have him walk on the 2 x 4. Which was easiest? Why? If there was a deep gully on one side of the 2 x 4, where would you choose to walk? Where would your parents tell you to walk? Why?

Choral Reading: Read the scripture on the lineboard with the children.

Story: "The Hike to Angle Canyon"
The four boys, Mike, John, Mark, and Brian, began their day hike. The previous week had been filled with instructions and warnings about the dangerous canyon overhangs. Each boy knew the dangers, but looked forward to seeing the beauties of the untamed country around Angle Canyon.
At first, the rolling hills were easy to climb. But the terrain became more difficult the higher they went. It was not long before they reached the beginning of Angle Canyon. The view was so beautiful that the boys scarcely noticed the drop of several hundred feet to the jagged rocks below.

John, Brian, and Mark remembered the advice they had been given and were careful about where they walked. But Mike, stepping back only slightly, continued to walk close to the edge. He encouraged his friends to join him so that they could see better; the rim was obviously safe. To prove his point he stepped closer to the edge, not seeing the dirt begin to crumble under his weight.

Discussion: What were the boys warned about? (The dangers of the canyon.) Why would someone warn them? (So they wouldn't get hurt.) Why do you think Mark didn't obey? (He forgot, or he didn't believe the warning.)

Obedience is an important thing to learn. We can all choose to obey or to disobey. Read the scripture again.

Singing Time Suggestions

"Choose the Right Way," 160
"Stand for the Right," 159

Conclusion

Tell the children that being obedient can help us avoid mistakes. It also teaches us trust and patience and can bring other blessings into our lives.

Our Bodies Are Special

Purpose

To help the children gain an understanding that their bodies are special and encourage them to take good care of their bodies.

Materials Needed

Picture of Salt Lake Temple (OQ433) or a picture of the temple of your choice, a chalkboard, chalk.

Preparation

Prepare two wordstrips: TEMPLE, YOU. Place the wordstrips on opposite sides of the chalkboard. Use the chalk to make a chart like the one shown in the game section of this lesson.

Print the following sentences on pieces of paper and randomly tape them under chairs.

1. Jared always watched appropriate television shows.
2. Staci always kept her hair washed and combed.
3. Jeff always wore clothes which kept the special parts of his body covered.
4. Mark spoke kindly to everyone he talked to.
5. Lisa always listened to conference and tried to do the things the prophet had spoken about.

Application

Discussion: Display the picture of the temple. Share your testimony that the temple is the house of the Lord. Help the children to see and appreciate the beauty of the temple. Help them to understand that there is a temple president who makes sure that the temple is cared for and run properly. He makes sure that the outside of the temple is clean and neat. Beautiful plants and flowers enhance its appearance. Of course the inside of the temple is clean and beautiful too. Describe the special, reverent feeling at the temple. The temple is filled with love. People must be obedient in order to go to the temple.

Scripture Reading: Have a student read 1 Corinthians 3:16–17.
What does this scripture compare our bodies to?
Our bodies are as sacred and special as a temple. Heavenly Father has called a temple president to be the steward of a temple, and he has given us stewardship over each of our bodies.

Game: Play the following matching game. Use chalk to draw lines to match the phrases. This will help the children to see the similarity between taking care of the temple and taking care of their bodies.

TEMPLE	YOU
1. Grounds kept clean	1. Obey commandments
2. Lovely flowers and plants	2. Love one another
3. Inside kept clean	3. Dress modestly
4. A feeling of love	4. Clean and groomed
5. Obedient may enter	5. Pure thoughts

Briefly review the phrases listed under "YOU." Point out that these are some of the things we must do in order to treat our bodies like a temple. Instruct the children to look under their chairs. Some of them will find slips of paper. One at a time, invite them to come up and read their paper. Have the group match each paper to a category listed under "YOU."

Singing Time Suggestions

"The Lord Gave Me a Temple," 153

Conclusion

Heavenly Father has entrusted us with the special gift of a body. We should take good care of it, for it is a temple.

People in the Scriptures

Purpose

To help us understand where people in the scriptures lived.

Materials Needed

World map, Bible, Book of Mormon.

Preparation

Prepare the following wordstrips: BIBLE, BOOK OF MORMON, ALMA, AMMON, BENJAMIN, DANIEL, DAVID, ESTHER, JOSEPH, LUKE, MARY, MORONI, MOSES, NEPHI, PAUL, RUTH, SARIAH (not all of these names need be used).

Prepare the display area by putting the wordstrip BIBLE in the upper left corner and the wordstrip BOOK OF MORMON in the upper right corner. Place all other wordstrips in the center (one under another but not in order).

Application

Discussion and Map: Show the Bible and the Book of Mormon and tell the children that these books contain stories about real people that lived a long time ago. These stories tell us things that the righteous people did and how Heavenly Father and Jesus helped them.

Who are some people we can read about in the Bible? (Take three or four appropriate answers.)

After people from the Bible have been named, point to the Middle East on your world map and explain that these people lived in this part of the world.

Who are some people we can read about in the Book of Mormon? (Take three or four answers.)

When the children are done naming the Book of Mormon people, show where the American continents are on the map and explain that

Book of Mormon people lived in this part of the world.

Activity: Take the world map down and tell the children that you have a list of some people whose stories are in the Bible and the Book of Mormon (indicate the wordstrips). Explain that you will give the group four clues and they must guess which person you are talking about and then tell whether their story can be found in the Bible or in the Book of Mormon.

Select one of the names and give the four clues. Ask which person you are talking about. After the person is identified, have a child move the wordstrip to the correct list (Bible or Book of Mormon). Do this for all the names you have chosen.

The clues for each wordstrip are:

1. Alma (1) was very wicked as a youth, (2) had an angel call him to repentance, (3) became the leader of the Church, (4) was the son of Alma the Elder.
2. Ammon (1) was a son of King Mosiah, (2) was a shepherd-servant of King Lamoni, (3) fought many thieves who were trying to steal the sheep, (4) was a great missionary to the Lamanites.
3. Benjamin (1) was a king that worked for a living, (2) wanted his people to live righteously, (3) gave a great speech to the people of Zarahemla, (4) had a tower built so the people could hear him.
4. Daniel (1) lived in ancient Babylon, (2) received wisdom and strength because of obedience to the commandments, (3) interpreted dreams and handwriting on the wall, (4) was saved from a den of lions because he kept the commandments and had faith.
5. David (1) was a shepherd, (2) played the harp and sang, (3) trusted and loved the Lord, (4) became a king in Israel.
6. Esther (1) was one of the most beautiful women in ancient Persia, (2) was chosen to be a wife of the Persian king because of her beauty, (3) fasted and prayed to solve a problem and then trusted in the Lord to help her, (4) saved the Jewish people from destruction.
7. Joseph (1) was the eldest son of Rachel and Jacob, (2) had eleven brothers, (3) had a coat of many colors, (4) was sold as a slave to Egypt but became a leader during a great famine.
8. Luke (1) was Roman, not Jewish, (2) was a doctor, (3) loved Jesus and knew that he was the Savior, (4) was a missionary companion to the Apostle Paul.
9. Mary (1) was visited by the angel Gabriel, (2) married a carpenter named Joseph, (3) was a cousin of John the Baptist's mother, (4) was the mother of Jesus.

10. Moroni (1) was the son of Mormon, (2) was the guardian of the golden plates, (3) wandered many years in the wilderness, (4) appeared to Joseph Smith.
11. Moses (1) was the son of Israelite slaves, (2) became a prince of Egypt, (3) parted the Red Sea, (4) talked to the Lord and received the Ten Commandments.
12. Nephi (1) was the son of Lehi and Sariah, (2) tried to be obedient to the Lord always, (3) led his father's family to the promised land.
13. Paul (1) was known in his early life as Saul, (2) tried to kill the followers of Jesus, (3) had a vision of the Savior on a trip to Damascus and repented of his sins, (4) wrote many of the Epistles and was a missionary to the Gentiles.
14. Ruth (1) was a Moabite woman, (2) was a daughter-in-law of Naomi, (3) gleaned wheat fields in Bethlehem, (4) married Boaz and had a son named Obed.
15. Sariah (1) was the mother of Nephi, (2) followed her husband into the wilderness to live in a tent, (3) left all her wealth to do what Heavenly Father commanded, (4) sailed in a ship to the promised land.

When the names have all been placed in the correct place compliment the children on how well they knew the scripture stories and challenge them to study the scriptures more so that they can understand about the people that lived so long ago.

Singing Time Suggestions

"The Books in the Old Testament," 114
"The Books in the New Testament," 116
"The Books in the Book of Mormon," 119

Conclusion

Display the world map again. Attach the wordstrip BIBLE to the map in the area of the Middle East. Remind the children that stories from the Bible took place in this part of the world. Attach the wordstrip BOOK OF MORMON to the correct part of the map and tell the children that the Book of Mormon stories took place on the American continents. If they study their scriptures they will learn more about the people of the scriptures.

Perfecting Yourself

Purpose

To gain an understanding that through learning of Christ and closely following his example we can perfect ourselves.

Materials Needed

Basketball, corkboard, picture of a basketball player.

Preparation

Cut two semi-circular arrows. When put together they should form a circle as well as point to each other. Label one INSTRUCTION and the other PRACTICE.

Print the six questions listed in the lesson on separate pieces of paper and number them.

Print the entire verse of 3 Nephi 12:48 on a lineboard. ("Therefore I would that ye should be perfect even as I, or your Father who is in heaven is perfect.")

Application

Discussion: Have a picture of a popular basketball player and a basketball displayed for all the students to see. Tell them to imagine that the famous ball player is coming to their homes. He is coming to teach them everything he knows about basketball: dribbling, passing, shooting, blocking, and much more. They watch him carefully and listen to everything he says. But that's not enough. He tells them that they have to practice everything he teaches them. So they begin to practice every day. He agrees to come and watch them practice. When he sees something they need to improve on, he stops them and gives more instruction. Then they practice again.

This continues day after day. He gives them the help they need, and they practice diligently each move he teaches them. He is helping each student to become a perfect basketball player.

Put the arrow labeled INSTRUCTION on the corkboard. The first step to becoming perfect in anything is receiving instruction from someone who is already experienced in that area. Put up the next arrow, labeled PRACTICE, to form the circle. The second part of perfection is to practice what has been taught. As we practice we receive more instruction to make us even better. We need to use that additional information as we continue to practice. Help the children to see that this is a cycle which repeats itself over and over until we become perfect.

Choral Reading: Display your lineboard and ask the children to read the verse with you.

Discussion: Pass out the prepared questions. Have the children take turns reading their question. Give the group a chance to talk about and discover the answer.

What have we been commanded to do? (Be perfect.)

Who is perfect? (Jesus and Heavenly Father.)

Who can give us instructions so we can be perfect too? (Jesus Christ.)

How can we receive this instruction? (Through the scriptures, prayer, and the prophets.)

What do we need to do after we receive this instruction? (Obey, or practice what we have learned.)

If we make a mistake what do we do? (Repent and go back to Christ for further instruction. Then be obedient once again.)

Singing Time Suggestions

"I'm Trying to Be like Jesus," 78
"I Want to Live the Gospel," 148
"I Will Follow God's Plan," 164

Conclusion

Refer back to your arrows. Point out that Jesus is the master teacher. He gives us instruction that helps us to be better. Then we practice what he has taught us. This is being obedient. If we continue this cycle of learning and obeying we will one day become perfect.

Plan of Salvation

Purpose

To help the children understand the plan of salvation and their part in it.

Preparation

Prepare six paper circles. Write one of the following on each circle: PRE-EXISTENCE, EARTH, SPIRIT WORLD, TELESTIAL, TERRESTRIAL, and CE-LESTIAL.
Prepare three wordstrips: BIRTH, DEATH, JUDGMENT.

Application

This activity is most effective when three people participate as teachers. Should this option not be available, one person can present the entire lesson. White clothing is also an effective element but equally optional.

Activity: Have a child put up the circle PRE-EXISTENCE.
First Teacher: Briefly tell the children how we all lived with Heavenly Father in the premortal existence. Talk about the war in heaven and their part in it. Let them know that they were on the "winning" side. Explain that when it was time for us to be born as mortals, we left Heavenly Father's kingdom and came to earth. Put the wordstrip BIRTH after the circle.
Have a child put up a circle EARTH.
Second Teacher: Tell the children that when we were born we forgot about the premortal existence. This needed to happen so that we could exercise faith and obedience. Briefly talk about why we wanted to gain mortal bodies and prove ourselves. Explain about adversity and temptation and how it can help us. Help them understand the Savior's important role. Put the wordstrip DEATH after EARTH.
Have a child place the circle SPIRIT WORLD on the board.
Third Teacher: Tell the children that after death and before resurrection we live in a place called the spirit world. Help the children under-

stand that this is not a spooky place but a place where many important things happen.

Put up the wordstrip JUDGMENT. Have a child help put up the three circles: TELESTIAL, TERRESTRIAL, and CELESTIAL.

Explain to the children that after we are judged for what we did on earth, we will enter one of the three kingdoms. Ask which kingdom Heavenly Father lives in. Tell the children that if they keep the commandments and follow the Savior's example, they will be able to enter the celestial kingdom because they will receive that blessing because of their faith and obedience and God's grace. Tell them that Heavenly Father wants us all to come and dwell with him because he loves us so much.

Singing Time Suggestions

"I Lived in Heaven," 4

Conclusion

Point to the circle marked PRE-EXISTENCE. Tell the children that before we were born we all lived with Heavenly Father. Point to EARTH and remind the children that this life is the time we have to learn many things and prove ourselves worthy to return to Heavenly Father. Point to the circle marked CELESTIAL and tell them that someday we can all live again with Heavenly Father in the celestial kingdom if we keep the commandments and do all that he wants us to do.

Prayer

Purpose

To teach the children the four parts of prayer and their order.

Materials Needed

Corkboard.

Preparation

Prepare eight simple drawings on pieces of paper: a girl, praying hands, a dress, a comb, a cup and bowl, a toothbrush, a coat, and a school bus.

Prepare four wordstrips: DEAR HEAVENLY FATHER; THANKS FOR BLESSINGS; ASK FOR NEEDS; IN THE NAME OF JESUS CHRIST, AMEN.

Application

Discussion: Mix up the pictures and put them up on the corkboard. Explain to your group that this is a silly story. It's told by pictures, but the pictures are all mixed up. Read the story the way it is, to show the group how silly it sounds. One by one have them help you put the pictures in the proper order. Read the story now. Explain that it now makes much more sense. For instance, you brush your teeth after eating, to get them clean. If you combed your hair before getting dressed, it could easily get messed up. These are things we do each morning, and the order we do them in is important.

Mix up your wordstrips and put them on the board. Explain that these wordstrips represent the four parts of prayer but they're not in the right order either. For our prayers to be reverent and pleasing to Heavenly Father we must follow the proper steps.

Sing or recite verse two of "I Pray in Faith," p. 14 in the *Children's Songbook*. Use this to guide the children in putting the wordstrips in order. Mix the wordstrips up again and see if the students can arrange them without the help of the song.

Discussion: Use the following topics to help the children more fully understand each part of prayer.

We must address Heavenly Father in a way which shows respect and endearment.

What blessings are we thankful for?

What needs can we pray for?

Why do we close in the name of Jesus Christ?

What does the term *amen* mean? (To agree or accept.)

Singing Time Suggestions

"I Pray in Faith," 14
"We Bow Our Heads," 25

Conclusion

Remove all the wordstrips and challenge the children to recall the four parts of prayer in the correct order.

Repentance

Purpose

To explain and help the children understand the process of complete repentance.

Materials Needed

Bandage.

Preparation

Prepare to tell "Jason's Watch."
Prepare four wordstrips: SORROW, CONFESSION, RESTITUTION, FORSAKE WRONG.

Application

Story: "Jason's Watch"

Kevin had lost his brother's watch; now he knew trouble was coming and he was going to be right in the middle of it. He could picture Jason's face when he found his watch missing. Kevin sighed and sat down on the porch.

Knowing that he shouldn't have taken the watch without asking didn't help at all. It had seemed a good idea at the time but now the only thing that seemed a good idea was staying as far from Jason as possible.

Later that night, when Jason couldn't find his watch, he spent a long time looking for it. Kevin watched quietly and even joined in the search, but he knew that no one would find it. It was somewhere down by the fishing pond.

When Jason asked about the watch, Kevin quietly said that he hadn't seen it. Now Kevin felt worse than ever; sometimes he even felt angry at Jason for leaving the watch where he could find it. Kevin felt as if he had a big heavy rock inside. Sometimes it hurt so much he felt like crying.

Discussion: Why do you think Kevin felt the way he did?

What does Kevin have to do to feel good again?

As you discuss the steps of repentance be sure to relate them to Kevin's story.

Place the wordstrip SORROW on the display area and explain that Kevin already feels sorrow for what he has done. He has taken the first step in the repentance process.

Next, put the CONFESSION wordstrip under SORROW.

What is confession? What must Kevin do to confess? Will it be easy? Will he feel better right away? Why is confession important?

Under CONFESSION place the wordstrip RESTITUTION.

What does restitution mean? What could Kevin do to make restitution? How will it help Kevin feel better?

End with the wordstrip FORSAKE WRONG.

What does it mean to try never to make the same mistake again? What would Kevin want to try to do?

Object Lesson: When we have a hurt on our bodies, even a small one, what should we do? (Clean it and put a bandage on it.) Show the children the bandage. What happens if we don't take care of a hurt? (It can become infected and make us more sick.) When we use repentance the right way, we can clean up our spiritual hurts and bandage them so they can heal and not cause other problems later.

Singing Time Suggestions

"Repentance," 98

Conclusion

Remind the children that repentance is like a bandage (show your bandage). It can help us heal our spiritual hurts when we (1) feel sorrow, (2) confess, (3) use restitution, and (4) forsake the wrong.

Resist Temptation and Become Stronger

Purpose

To help each child understand that resisting temptation makes us stronger, and draws us closer to Jesus Christ.

Materials Needed

Corkboard, picture of the Savior (OQ572).

Preparation

Prepare three wordstrips: JESUS CHRIST, SATAN, YOU.

Cut out nine rectangles of construction paper to represent bricks. Label each one with a temptation that the children in your group may have to deal with. (Example: Johnny's friends tried to get him to smoke a cigarette.)

Print the first part of James 1:12 on a lineboard. ("Blessed is the man that endureth temptation: for when he is tried, he shall receive the crown of life.")

Application

Game: Play a quick game of "Who am I?" Give the following information and invite the children to guess who it is.

When I was hungry, Satan tempted me to turn a stone into bread.

Satan took me to a high pinnacle of the temple and tempted me to throw myself off and have the angels catch me.

Satan tempted me to worship him by offering me all the kingdoms and power of the world.

Who am I? (Jesus Christ.) Display the picture of Christ. Explain that Satan tried to tempt him many different ways, but Jesus always resisted his temptations, and did the right things. Bear your testimony of Christ's great power. Tell the children that he gave us the key to having strength over Satan. That key is resisting temptation.

70

Role-Playing: Place the wordstrips on the corkboard with YOU in the center, and JESUS CHRIST and SATAN on opposite sides. Divide your students into small groups. Give a paper brick to each group and give them a couple of minutes to prepare to role-play their situation for everyone. Explain that they need to show the best way to resist their temptation.

Begin as soon as the groups appear to be ready. After each group successfully shows how to resist their temptation take the paper brick and place it between the wordstrips YOU and SATAN. Continue to put the bricks on the corkboard to fashion a wall. Explain that as the children resist temptation they become stronger and begin to build a wall between Satan and themselves. Contrast this by pointing out that if they follow Satan's temptations they become weaker, and Satan uses the bricks to build a wall between them and Jesus Christ.

Choral Reading: Display your lineboard and invite the children to read James 1:12 with you.

Singing Time Suggestions

"Dare to Do Right," 158
"I Will Be Valiant," 162

Conclusion

Remind your students that if they will resist temptation they will become stronger. They will also grow closer to Jesus Christ.

Resisting Temptation

Purpose

To help students discover that it is better to resist temptation than to have to repent.

Materials Needed

Picture: Jesus the Christ (OQ572).

Preparation

Prepare to tell "Jake and the Mud Puddle."
Prepare one wordstrip: HEAVENLY HOME.
Print on a lineboard the first part of 3 Nephi 27:19. ("And no unclean thing can enter into his kingdom.")
Print the following situations on slips of paper and seal them in separate envelopes.

1. James didn't have enough money to buy a toy glider so he stole it from the store. He tore open the package and used it and then felt guilty.
2. Nancy borrowed her mother's necklace without asking. When she wore it the clasp broke.
3. Ted thought his friend wasn't playing a game fairly, so he pushed him. His friend fell and chipped a tooth.
4. Mary wanted her friends to like her, so she lied by telling them she was going to have a big party.
5. Charlie and his dad were going to a ball game. Charlie promised he would mow the lawn first. He played with his friends instead and didn't get home until it was time to go to the game.

Application

Story: "Jake and the Mud Puddle"
Jake jumped off the school bus. It had been raining all day, and there

were big mud puddles all the way up the dirt lane to his house. The mud and water seemed too much for Jake to resist. Stomp! Stomp! Squish! Squash! Splash! Jake got into every puddle between the bus stop and his house. What fun it seemed to be!

Jake reached his home and began to open the door. Mother opened it first and blocked the doorway. She didn't say a word but looked down at his muddy shoes. Jake knew what she was thinking. He couldn't come into their clean house with mud all over him. He would have to clean up first. Silently Mother handed Jake an old butter knife. Sitting down on the top steps of the porch he began the slow task of scraping all the caked mud off his shoes.

Jake's little brother turned the television on and Jake could hear the music from his favorite show beginning. Jake continued to scrape. Those puddles didn't seem to be nearly as much fun now.

Finally his shoes were clean. His job still wasn't finished though. Mother quietly took the butter knife from him and handed him a broom. Looking back over his shoulder, Jake saw the muddy dirt all over the porch. So he began to sweep. The smell of warm, chocolate chip cookies teased his nose. Mother always baked cookies on rainy days. Jake's stomach growled, reminding him how hungry he was. He swept harder than ever and wished he'd never gotten near those puddles.

He finished the porch, and handed Mother the broom. He saw her eyes travel down to the cuffs of his pants. Sighing, he said, "I'll go change." Jake rolled the edges of his pants up and went upstairs. By the time he'd changed his pants and put his dirty clothes in the hamper his favorite television show was almost over.

Jake took a bite of a cookie as he looked out of the big window. No, those mud puddles were definitely not as much fun as they had appeared to be.

Discussion: What did Jake do wrong?
   Why couldn't he go into his house?
   What did he have to do?
   Did it take a long time?
   What do you think Jake will do next time?

Choral Reading: As a group, read the verse printed on the lineboard.

Discussion: Display the picture of Christ and place the HEAVENLY HOME wordstrip under it. Explain that we are all trying to return to our heavenly home. There are wonderful things waiting for us there. (Better things even than Jake's favorite show or the chocolate chip cookies.)

Because our heavenly home is so special, we can only enter in if we are spiritually clean. Repenting when we disobey keeps us clean.

Buzz Session: Divide the students up into small groups. Pass out a prepared envelope to each group. Explain that they each have been given a situation of someone who has been disobedient. Their job is to figure out all the things the individual would have to do to completely repent.

When they're finished have each group share their situations and solutions. Be sure to add any steps of repentance they may have overlooked.

Singing Time Suggestions

"Choose the Right Way," 160
"Quickly I'll Obey," 197

Conclusion

Tell your students that you'd like to see what they have discovered in this lesson by asking them just two questions: Is it easier to resist temptation or to repent? Why?

Responsibility for Actions

Purpose

To teach the children the importance of admitting when we are wrong.

Materials Needed

A clear glass jar with a mouth large enough for your hand to fit through; a gumball.

Preparation

Print on index cards the four story situations from the lesson. Write the answer choices on separate slips of paper.

Print the following part of Ether 12:37 on a lineboard: "And because thou hast seen thy weakness thou shalt be made strong."

Application

Activity: Use the following stories (or some of your own choosing) to help the children understand the importance of accepting responsibility for their own actions. Invite four children to stand in front and hand them each an answer choice paper. Read the story from your index card. Next have the four children read the choices. Then involve the group in helping to eliminate the wrong choices first. Some choices may seem silly. Ask if we sometimes make silly excuses for ourselves. Other choices blame someone else. Ask the children if it is easier to blame others than to admit we were wrong. This will help channel them to the right answer.

1. Joel was riding his bike very fast down the bumpy path. His brother called to him. About the same time, there was a rock on the path. His bike wheel hit it and he crashed to the ground. Some of the spokes were broken out of the wheel. His knees were skinned and he was very angry.

Why did Joel crash on his bike?
   A. A rock suddenly appeared on the ground.
   B. His brother called to him.
   C. His bike was old.
   D. He was going too fast and didn't watch where he was going.

(If Joel blames something or someone else he will never learn to be careful on his bike.)

2.   Susie hated math. She didn't like to do the homework. And she didn't like to listen to the teacher in class. She got a D on her report card. She didn't think it was fair, because her friend got an A.

Why did Susie get a D in math?
   A. The teacher liked her friend better.
   B. The teacher gave too much homework.
   C. The class was boring.
   D. Susie didn't study hard enough.

(If Susie blames others she will never realize that she needs to work harder in school.)

3.   Randy wanted to be on the basketball team. He went to the practices every day after school. He told jokes and did silly things. Everyone laughed at him, except the coach. The coach finally told Randy he couldn't be on the team.

Why did Randy get put off the basketball team?
   A. Randy wasn't a good basketball player.
   B. The coach didn't like him.
   C. The other kids were goofing off.
   D. Randy didn't behave or pay attention at practice.

(If Randy blames others, he will never learn it is important to act appropriately.)

4.   Judy is going swimming with some friends. Her parents tell her to be home by three o'clock. Judy and her friends were still having fun when it was time to leave, so they stayed longer. On the way home they had ice cream. Judy didn't get back until five. Her parents grounded her for two weeks. Judy was mad because she didn't think it was fair.

Why did Judy get grounded?
   A. Her parents were mean.
   B. Her friends wanted to stay longer.
   C. The ice cream man was too slow.
   D. Judy didn't come home when she was supposed to.

(If Judy doesn't accept the responsibility for her actions, she'll never learn to obey the rules.)

Object Lesson: Place a gumball in the bottom of a jar. Reach in to get it. Make a fist around it and try and pull your hand out of the jar. With your hand clenched around the gumball, it cannot fit back out of the jar opening. Explain that you can't get your hand out of the jar and ask why. The children will quickly tell you to let go of the gumball and your hand will easily slip out. Demonstrate this for them.
   Liken this to admitting when we are wrong. If we keep hanging on, trying to prove we're right, we will find ourselves in constant trouble.

Choral Reading and Discussion: Read the scripture on the lineboard as a group. Use the following questions to develop a discussion.
   What does "thou hast seen thy weakness" mean? (To admit that we have been wrong.)
   If we are willing to go to Heavenly Father in prayer and admit that we have been wrong, what two things does he promise us? (That our weakness will be made strong, that we will live with him again.)
   Point out what wonderful blessings these are.

Singing Time Suggestions

"Repentance," 98

Conclusion

In order to be strong, we must first realize where we are weak. If we refuse to see our error, we may rob ourselves of wonderful blessings of strength and of eternity with Heavenly Father.

Reverence

Purpose

How we touch, hold, or treat things helps us remember to be reverent.

Preparation

Prepare several lists of things we should show reverence for. Examples include: pets, friends, family, trees and plants, scriptures, teachers, a church building, ourselves, school buildings, animals, or any other appropriate idea.

Prepare a wordstrip: REVERENCE IS LOVE.

Arrange for two or three children to bring a "treasure" and be prepared to tell about why it is so special.

Prepare the chalkboard for the discussion by writing "OURS" on the top left side and "HEAVENLY FATHER'S" on the top right.

Application

Sharing Activity: Ask each previously assigned child to show their "treasure" and tell why it is special to them.

Chalkboard Discussion: When each treasure has been talked about, ask the other children to name their own special "treasures." List these on the board under OURS.

How do we treat things that we treasure? Do we hold them differently? Do we speak in a different way about them?

How do we want other people to hold our treasure? Do we want them to be careful or careless?

Tell the children that how we treat our treasures is a way of showing respect or reverence. Heavenly Father has given us many things that he treasures. Discuss some of the treasures that Heavenly Father allows us to take care of. (Earth, scriptures, family, home, church, other people, ourselves, etc.) List these on the board under HEAVENLY FATHER'S. (For very young children you may want to use pictures for this part. These can be held by the children.)

How does Heavenly Father want us to take care of his treasures?

How can we show respect or reverence for what Heavenly Father loves?

Buzz Session: Give each group one of the prepared lists and have them discuss how we can show reverence for the items listed.

After a few minutes, have someone from each group share what they decided from their discussion.

Discussion: Post the wordstrip REVERENCE IS LOVE. Tell the children that how they touch, hold, or treat the things Heavenly Father has given them can help them to be a reverent person. When we show reverence for Heavenly Father and his many gifts, we are showing our love for him.

Singing Time Suggestions

"Reverence Is Love," 31
"I Feel My Savior's Love," 74

Conclusion

Point to the wordstrip and remind the children that when we show reverence for Heavenly Father and his many gifts we are showing our love for him.

The Sacrament

Purpose

To help students gain an understanding that we draw nearer to Christ through being obedient to our sacrament covenants.

Materials Needed

Book of Mormon, transparency marker, tissue paper, picture of the Savior (OQ572).

Preparation

Print the last part of Moroni 4:3 on a lineboard. ("Always remember him, and keep his commandments which he hath given them, that they may always have his Spirit to be with them.")

Prepare a picture of Christ (OQ572) by covering it with three layers of tissue paper. Secure tissue paper at the top with paper clips or tape.

Print the following message on a small piece of paper: "Don't play with Jake at break time or you won't have any friends. Pass it on."

Prepare to tell "Mark's Choices."

Application

Discussion: Have a child read Moroni 4:3 (the sacrament prayer). Ask the children where they have heard these same words. (When the sacrament is blessed each Sunday.)

Display the prepared lineboard. Explain that there is a special part of that prayer that you want to talk about. Read the lineboard. What are the two things we promise to do in the sacrament prayer? (Always remember him and keep his commandments.) Underline these portions on the lineboard.

If we do those two things, what does Jesus promise us? (That we will always have his Spirit to be with us.) This is a very special promise. Explain that there is a story which shows just how this works.

Story: "Mark's Choices" (Display the prepared picture of Christ.)

Mark was eight years old. He had just been baptized and he had a testimony of Jesus Christ. Point out the prepared picture of Christ. Ask the group if they can tell who the picture is of. (Press the paper flat against the picture so that the image of Christ is slightly detected.) Explain that this was like Mark's early testimony of Jesus. He wanted his testimony to grow. His father told him that if he followed the instruction in the sacrament prayer his testimony would grow very strong.

When Mark partook of the bread and water that special Sunday after his baptism, he really promised to remember Jesus, and to keep his commandments.

The next day he went to school. Just before the break time the boy sitting next to him passed a note to Mark, and this is what it said: (have a boy read the prepared note). Mark started to pass the note on to the next person in the row, but suddenly he thought of the sacrament prayer. What would Jesus do? He looked at the note in his hand and crumpled it up. Mark invited Jake to play basketball with him during the break. The kids would probably tease him for a while, but when he thought of Jesus it didn't matter. In fact it made Mark feel closer to Jesus. (Remove one sheet of tissue paper and point out that you can now see the picture a little more clearly.)

Later that week, Mark was invited to go with his friends to the amusement park. Mark loved the amusement park, especially the roller coaster. He was disappointed when he asked his parents if he could go. His father said they all had to work in the garden on Saturday to get the vegetables harvested. Mark started to complain, hoping his father would change his mind. Suddenly he remembered Jesus. He knew Jesus would have obeyed without complaining. So Mark did his best to hide his disappointment. He was a little surprised when a special feeling came to him. He really could feel the Savior's love. (Remove another sheet of tissue paper, and help the students to see how clear the picture is becoming.)

A week later Mark went to the school carnival. He was standing in line at the dunking booth. When an older boy in front of him left, Mark noticed the boy had left his watch. It was a really nice one. Mark had always wanted a watch. The boy would never realize that Mark had taken it. As he picked the watch up, he thought about Jesus. He knew what to do. Quickly he ran to catch up with the boy and return the watch. That night as Mark lay in bed, he thought about his testimony. A warm feeling spread throughout his body. He felt so close to Jesus that it was as if he could almost see him. (Remove the final sheet of tissue paper.)

Singing Time Suggestions

"The Sacrament," 72
"I'm Trying to Be like Jesus," 78

Conclusion

Reread Moroni 4:3. Remind the students that as we try to remember the Savior and do what he would want us to, his Spirit will always be with us. We will feel him and his love just as Mark did.

Scriptures

Purpose

To illustrate that the scriptures teach us about Jesus Christ so we can be more like him.

Materials Needed

Seven pictures: the birth of Jesus (OQ116), boy Jesus in the temple (OQ500), Jesus blessing Jairus' daughter (OQ231), Jesus blessing the children (OQ140), stilling the storm (OQ139), the Crucifixion (OQ505), Mary and the resurrected Lord (OQ186); several types of books (cookbook, auto repair, gardening).

Preparation

Print the entire verse of John 5:39 on a lineboard. ("Search the scriptures; for in them ye have eternal life: and they are they which testify of me.")
Prepare to tell the following stories of the life of Christ:

1. His birth
2. Teaching at the temple when he was twelve
3. Blessing Jairus' daughter
4. Beckoning the children to come to him
5. Calming the sea
6. His crucifixion
7. His resurrection

Application

Scripture Stories: Pass out the pictures of Jesus Christ's life to several class members. Instruct them to listen carefully as you tell some stories. When they recognize that their picture goes with the story you're telling they are to come and hold the picture up for the whole class to see. Tell the stories in order. Be sure to point out important things we learn about Christ in each story. (Example: he had great love for others.) Ask where these stories come from. (The scriptures.) Remind the children that the scriptures teach us about Jesus Christ.

Object Lesson: Show the group the various books you've brought. There are many different types of books. If you wanted a recipe for cookies, you would look in a cookbook. If you wanted information on growing vegetables you would read a gardening book. It's important to use a book that will give you the right information. Heavenly Father has given us the scriptures to help us. By reading them we can learn about Jesus and how to be more like him.

Singing Time Suggestions

"Seek the Lord Early," 108
"Search, Ponder, and Pray," 109

Conclusion

Display the lineboard. Invite the children to read the verse with you. Encourage them to read the scriptures every day.

Scriptures Provide Answers

Purpose

To encourage students to use scriptures to resolve personal problems.

Materials Needed

Transparency marker.

Preparation

Print the following scriptural references on slips of paper:

1. Proverbs 21:21 (word 9 in the verse goes in the blank)
2. John 6:29 (word 2)
3. Doctrine and Covenants 1:37 (word 1)
4. 2 Timothy 3:15 (word 11)
5. Alma 37:35 (word 6)
6. Mormon 3:21 (word 6)
7. John 3:16 (word 13)
8. Moroni 7:42 (word 6)
9. 1 John 4:19 (word 2)

Print the following phrase on the lineboard.

All questions in ____(1)____ can be ____(2)____ as we ____(3)____ the ____(4)____. We also ____(5)____ to ____(6)____ in Jesus, the ____(7)____ of God and have ____(8)____ in his ____(9)____ for us.

Print Doctrine and Covenants 88:63 on the reverse side of the lineboard. ("Draw near unto me and I will draw near unto you; seek me diligently and ye shall find me; ask, and ye shall receive; knock, and it shall be opened unto you.")

Prepare to tell "Susan Finds an Answer."

Application

Game: Show the puzzle to the children and tell them that you need their help to find out what it means. Divide the previously prepared slips of paper among the children.

After giving them enough time to look up the scriptural references, have the children read their entire scripture to everyone. Then have them tell what the missing word is. You (or an older child) may then fill in the missing word.

When the entire message is completed have someone read it aloud.

Tell the children that life is filled with puzzles or problems. Express to them how searching the scriptures can help us find answers that will keep us close to the Savior.

Choral Reading: Turn the lineboard over to present the scripture. Ask the children to think about the scripture as you read it. Read Doctrine and Covenants 88:63. Tell the children to read with you as you read the scripture again.

Story: "Susan Finds an Answer"

Ever since Susan's family had moved to Marston, she had felt unhappy and lonely. Before, when they lived in Jonestown, she had many friends and had never felt this way. Mother told her that soon she would make new friends and then she wouldn't be so sad.

One evening Susan and her older sister Gina were doing the dishes and talking about how Susan felt.

"Gina, I miss my old friends a lot. When will I ever find new friends?"

Gina thought for a moment as they quietly finished the last few dishes. Then she asked Susan to come to her room. When they were seated comfortably on the bed, Gina took out her scriptures and carefully looked through the pages.

"Brother Thomas, my Sunday School teacher, told us that we can find answers for every problem in the scriptures. I'd like to read you the scripture he used."

Gina finally found the scripture she was looking for and read, "'Draw near unto me and I will draw near unto you; seek me diligently and ye shall find me; ask, and ye shall receive; knock, and it shall be opened unto you' (D&C 88:63).

"Brother Thomas told us that as we try to come closer to Heavenly Father, by reading our scriptures and praying we will be able to find the answers we need. Susan, if you think and pray, you will know what you need to do."

Gina gave Susan a big hug and told her that she would help her all she could.

That night, Susan looked up *Happiness* in her Topical Guide and found a special scripture in John. "If ye know these things, happy are ye if ye do them" (John 13:17). Later, Susan prayed to Heavenly Father for ways to solve her problem. As she thought, she knew the best way to get closer to Heavenly Father was to act like Jesus and help other people.

All that week Susan did things that helped other people. At home she tried harder to help without being asked. At school she helped younger children reach the drinking fountain and she helped the girl sitting next to her with her math. At church she tried to sing her very best and listen to the lesson.

Before she knew it she felt less lonely and felt closer to Heavenly Father and Jesus. As she helped other people and prayed for Heavenly Father to help her, her unhappy feelings went away and she felt happier to be with her new friends in Marston.

Discussion: What did Susan's older sister do to help Susan with her problem? (She listened and helped her find a scripture.)

What did Susan do to help herself be less lonely? (She tried to be more like Jesus.)

What did she do to be more like Jesus? (She helped other people.)

How did the scriptures help her? (They helped her understand what she could do to be happier.)

Singing Time Suggestions

"Seek the Lord Early," 108

Conclusion

Have all the children together reread the scripture aloud. If you desire, you may bear your testimony about scriptures.

Seasons

Purpose

To help the children understand and enjoy the seasons of the year.

Materials Needed

Four pictures, each depicting one of the four seasons: spring, summer, autumn, winter.

Application

Place the four pictures of the seasons on the display area. Tell the children that each season of the year is different from the others. Tell them that today we are going to describe the seasons in many ways.

Answer each of the following questions for each season and list student responses under the appropriate picture. Compare answers as you go.

What are the four seasons?

What does the land look like?

What are the plants doing? If you have a garden, what are you doing with it?

What are the animals doing?

What are some things you like to do?

What are some holidays we celebrate during this time?

What time of year is it right now?

Heavenly Father loves us very much. He gave us the seasons of the year to enjoy. Each season is special in its own way. Even though we may enjoy one time of year more than another, we can still be grateful for and learn to appreciate every time of the year.

Singing Time Suggestions

"I Think the World Is Glorious," 230
"My Heavenly Father Loves Me," 228
Seasonal songs, 238 through 249

Conclusion

Tell the children that this is a special time of year and tell them that, if they look, they will see many exciting and beautiful things that Heavenly Father has prepared for them.

Seeking the Lord's Blessings

Purpose

To teach the students that asking for needed blessings is an important part of prayer.

Materials Needed

Chalkboard, chalk.

Preparation

Select prayerfully two individuals (teachers, students, or guests) to share a personal experience which illustrates receiving blessings that were asked for through prayer.

Read Daniel, Chapter 6, and be prepared to tell the story of Daniel in the lions' den in your own words.

Application

Sharing Activity: Introduce your speakers and explain that they each had a special experience with prayer that they would like to share with your group.

Discussion: Following the talks, conduct a brief discussion pointing out that asking for needed blessings is an important element of prayer. Use specific examples from the talks to reinforce this.

Scripture Story: There are many stories in the scriptures that teach us about people who have prayerfully sought for Heavenly Father's help. Daniel is a wonderful example. (Tell his story in your own words.)

What help did Daniel need?

What did he do?

How was his prayer answered?

Chalkboard Activity: Explain that we may not all be endangered by fierce lions, but we do have needs each day. Tell the class that they have three minutes to list as many ideas of what they can ask for in prayer as they can. You will write the answers on the chalkboard. Start the timer and begin. If they slow down, give them some key questions.

What needs do you have at school?

What help could you use in sports?

Does your family need any special help?

Congratulate them for fine thinking. Express to them Heavenly Father's desire to help them with their needs. Through prayer they can ask for his help.

Singing Time Suggestions

"I Pray in Faith," 14

"I Need My Heavenly Father," 18

Conclusion

Have a child read 2 Nephi 32:9.

Service

Purpose

To teach children that we show our love for the Savior through serving others.

Materials Needed

Dominoes, pencils, staples, stapler, picture of the Savior (OQ572).

Preparation

Cut red and white paper strips to make a paper chain. Each child will need one of each color.

Cut a row of large paper dolls. Write "love" on the first arm of the first doll, write "service" on its other arm. Label the entire row of dolls in this manner.

Display the picture of Christ during the entire lesson.

Application

Object Lesson: Line up a row of dominoes. Let a child come and push the first domino down. It will knock the rest of the row over too. Explain that even though the first domino was the only one that was touched, it pushed the second one over, which knocked the third one down. It continued in this way until the entire row fell.

Display the row of paper dolls. Explain that love and service work similarly to the dominoes. Liken the paper dolls to ourselves. As we learn about Jesus we grow to love him. We begin to feel so much love that we show it by helping, or serving, someone else. That person feels the love that your service brought to them, and their love becomes so great that they in turn serve another. This can continue on and on without end.

Tell the students to raise their hands if—

1. They would feed Jesus if he was hungry.
2. They would give him something warm to wear if he was cold.
3. They would help him if he was sick or tired.

Choral Reading: As a group, read the verse on the lineboard. Help the children to understand its meaning. Jesus tells us that when we serve others it is as if we are serving him. If we love Jesus we will serve others. This follows a plan of action just like the dominoes.

Activity: Pass out the paper strips and pencils to the children. Tell them that the white paper represents their love for Jesus, and the red paper represents their acts of service. Instruct them to write their names on each of the strips. Use a stapler to link them together until the whole chain is finished. Hang it up for the children to see.

Singing Time Suggestions

"I Feel My Savior's Love," 74
"When He Comes Again," 82
"Kindness Begins with Me," 145

Conclusion

Refer back to the paper chain. Point out that the love of Christ can bind us together. If we help each other and work together, great things can happen.

Spirituality

Purpose

To teach students that prayer, the scriptures, and obedience are the tools we must use to help us return to our Heavenly Father.

Materials Needed

Transparency marker, string, masking tape, plastic straw, several balloons.

Preparation

Print HEAVENLY HOME on a lineboard.
Print Matthew 7:7 on the reverse side of the lineboard. ("Ask, and it shall be given you; seek, and ye shall find; knock, and it shall be opened unto you.")

Application

Object Lesson: Display the poster and explain that our goal in life is to return to live with Jesus and Heavenly Father. Have one of the children help you in an illustration. Blow up a balloon and give it to the child. Have them hold the end so the air doesn't escape. Then direct them to aim the balloon at the poster and let it go. The balloon will whirl about in all directions missing completely its goal of HEAVENLY HOME. Let the child try it again. Remind them of where their target is.

Spend a brief moment to explain that the balloon had a lot of energy but nothing to direct its course to the HEAVENLY HOME.

Next attach one end of string to the poster. Have someone at the other side of the room hold the string taut. Feed that end of the string through a plastic straw. (The straw serves as a vehicle powered by the air in the balloon to carry the balloon to the poster.) Blow up another balloon and once again have the child hold the end. Using tape, fasten the balloon to the straw. Allow the child to release the balloon. This time it will swiftly follow a direct course along the string to the poster.

94

Discussion: Explain that the balloon needed certain tools to help channel its energy in the correct direction.

What were these tools? (Tape, straw, and string.)

We also need to use special tools to channel our energy into a course which will return us to our Heavenly Father. These tools are prayer, the scriptures, and obedience.

Choral Reading: Turn the lineboard over and invite the children to read Matthew 7:7 with you.

Singing Time Suggestions

"Search, Ponder, and Pray," 109

Conclusion

Underline *ask*, *seek*, and *knock*. Relate these to prayer, scripture study, and obedience. By using these tools we can return to our heavenly home where the door will be opened to us.

Temple Preparedness

Purpose

To teach the children the things they should do now to prepare them to go to the temple.

Preparation

Prepare six wordstrips: WORD OF WISDOM; KIND TO FAMILY; MORALLY CLEAN; FOLLOWING THE PROPHET; TESTIMONY OF CHRIST; and RE-PENTANCE. (Objects or pictures can be used to symbolize ideas for small children. Example: a piece of fruit for the Word of Wisdom.)

Prepare a suitcase packed with a towel, a swimsuit, sunglasses, and a deflated beach ball.

Application

Game: Display the packed suitcase. Explain that you can usually tell where someone is going by what they have packed in their suitcase. Show the children the items in the suitcase one by one. Ask them where that person would be going. (To the beach.)

Instruct the students that they are going someplace in the world. They must figure out where they are going by the items packed in the suitcase. Tell them you will give them clues, so they'll know what to pack. Remind them to keep the answer a secret until the game is over. As each clue is given allow the child to place the appropriate wordstrip in the suitcase. Briefly discuss each subject.

Clues
1. You know that Jesus is the Christ. You also know that The Church of Jesus Christ of Latter-day Saints is the true church. What do you have? (A testimony.)
2. You always listen to general conference. You enjoy hearing the President of the Church speak and you do those things that he says to. Who do you follow? (The prophet.)

96

3. You never raise your voice to your brothers and sisters. You always share. How do you treat your family? (Kindly.)
4. You treat your body like a temple, keeping it clean inside and out. What is this called? (Moral cleanliness.)
5. When you make a mistake, you tell Heavenly Father how sorry you are. You try to make up for your error. You try never to do it again. What is this? (Repentance.)

After all the clues are given ask the children where they are going. (To the temple.)

Singing Time Suggestions

"I Love to See the Temple," 95

Conclusion

Conclude by reversing the game. Ask them to recall the items which were packed. This will reinforce these elements in their memories.

Testimony

Purpose

To teach the children the different elements of a testimony.

Materials Needed

A corkboard; pictures: Jesus the Christ (OQ572), Prophet Joseph Smith (OQ002), meetinghouse (OQ357), Ezra Taft Benson (OQ576).

Preparation

Prepare a wordstrip: MY TESTIMONY.
Prepare from construction paper the parts of a house: foundation, walls (the structure itself), window, door, and roof.

Application

Activity: Put up the wordstrip MY TESTIMONY. Explain that building a testimony is like building a house.

What is the first thing you need to build on your house? (Hint: this is something that keeps the floors off the ground.)

A foundation. (Place the foundation on the corkboard.) The foundation must be very strong because it holds up the whole house. Display some sand, and concrete or rock.

Which item would be the strongest and best to use for the foundation?

The rock or concrete. (Display the picture of Jesus Christ on the corkboard.) Christ is the foundation of our testimonies. He is strong and powerful and will always support us. (Sing together "The Wise Man and the Foolish Man," p. 281 in the *Children's Songbook.)*

What is the next thing our house needs?

Walls. (Put the walls onto the foundation of the house.) Walls are very important because they give us a secure place to live. (Put the picture of

Joseph Smith next to Christ's picture.) A testimony of Joseph Smith is like having walls on our house. There is security in knowing that he was the prophet who restored the gospel.

What is our house missing?

A roof. (Place the roof on the house.) A roof protects us from the rain and the other elements. It keeps our house warm and safe. Having a testimony that The Church of Jesus Christ of Latter-day Saints is the only true church is just as important as the roof on a house. Other churches have good people in them but only have part of the gospel, and that would be like a roof with holes in it. We all know what happens when a roof has a hole in it. It leaks! (Place a picture of a church meetinghouse next to the other pictures.)

Our house is still missing something. What is it?

Windows and a door. (Put the windows and door on the house.) They help us to see what's outside. We can be better prepared by this. For instance, if we see that it is raining, we can take an umbrella. (Display the picture of our prophet.) A testimony of our prophet is like the windows and doors of a house. Through revelation from Heavenly Father, the prophet can prepare us for the latter days.

Explain to the children that just as each part of the house is vital, so is each part of our testimony.

Singing Time Suggestions

"On a Golden Springtime," 88
"The Church of Jesus Christ," 77
"Latter-day Prophets," 134

Conclusion

Remove the pictures and see if the class can remember the parts of a testimony. Associate it with the parts of a house and they will easily recall it.

Testimony—Steps in Gaining One

Purpose

To help the children understand how to gain a testimony.

Materials Needed

Hoe, watering can, bottle or package of seeds.

Preparation

Prepare five wordstrips: DESIRE, FAITH, PRAYER/SCRIPTURES, NEGA-TIVES, BELIEF.

Prepare to tell "Steve's Testimony."

Application

Discussion and Object Lesson: Bring out the hoe, watering can, and seeds, and tell the children that you are getting ready to plant a garden. At appropriate times during the object lesson refer to the hoe, can, and seeds.

Ask if anyone has ever planted a garden. What is the first thing we must do to plant a garden? (Prepare the soil.) What do we do next? (Plant the seed.) What does a seed need to grow? (Sunshine and water.) What happens if the soil is loosened and the seed gets plenty of water and sunshine? (It will start to grow.) Are we done with our garden? What else do we have to do? (Keep it free of weeds.) When all these things are done what will we have? (A good harvest.)

Tell the children that gaining a testimony is very much like planting a garden. First we must prepare. How do we prepare the soil? (Put up wordstrip DESIRE.) What seed do we need to plant? (Put up wordstrip FAITH.) What is the water and sunshine that helps a testimony grow? (Put up wordstrip PRAYER/SCRIPTURES.) What are the spiritual weeds that must be gotten rid of? (Ask for specific answers, then post NEGATIVES.) What is the harvest? (Put up wordstrip BELIEF.)

Story: "Steve's Testimony"

Steve often saw other people bear their testimonies and he wondered what if felt like. He had prayed a little but still didn't feel that he had a testimony.

He remembered hearing about the seed of faith in a family home evening. If Heavenly Father wanted him to have a testimony, then Steve had to believe that he could gain a testimony. He would have faith.

Every night before he went to bed Steve read some scriptures and prayed to Heavenly Father about his testimony. Days turned into weeks as Steve continued to take care of that seed of faith about his testimony. Even though he didn't feel any different he knew that Heavenly Father would give him that blessing if he just kept trying.

One fast Sunday, testimony meeting started and Steve listened carefully to the many testimonies that were given. More than anything else he wanted to stand and have a testimony to bear, to know that the gospel was true. Then he realized that he *could* stand and tell about his blessings.

As he stood, a feeling of happiness came to him and he was able to speak the words he had worked so hard to earn. "I know Heavenly Father loves me. I know that he answers prayers. I believe in the gospel of Jesus Christ." Steve had a testimony.

Singing Time Suggestions

"I Know My Father Lives," 5

Conclusion

Tell the boys and girls that Heavenly Father wants them to have a testimony but they must earn it. Reread the steps to gaining a testimony. Challenge the children to seek and earn their own testimony.

Transgression

Purpose

To illustrate that transgression keeps us from experiencing the light of Christ.

Materials Needed

A plant which has been removed from all light for several days, flannelboard.

Preparation

Prepare the following flannelboard pictures: a large sun, a boy, several dark clouds.

Print the last part of John 8:12 on a lineboard. ("I am the light of the world: he that followeth me shall not walk in darkness, but shall have the light of life.")

Arrange for a guest speaker to share a personal experience and testimony which would illustrate the need for the light of Christ in our lives.

Application

Flannelboard Story: Place the large sun on your flannelboard above the little boy. Talk about all the things the sun does for us. (If we're wet it dries us, if we're cold it warms us, it gives us light so we can see.) Place a cloud over part of the sun and ask the children what happens if clouds begin to cover the sun. (It gets darker and colder.) Tell them that the sun is still there but we can't see it or feel it as much because the clouds are blocking it.

Point out that the light of Christ is very similar to the sun. It warms us. It comforts us. It also gives us the light to see spiritually so we are better guided in our decisions.

When we make a wrong choice, or transgress, it's like a cloud that blocks the fullness of the light of Christ. If we continued to transgress without repenting, that cloud would eventually completely conceal his light from us. He would still be there, but our transgressions would have put a barrier between his light and ourselves.

Show how this works on the flannelboard by continuing to put clouds over the sun. Refer to each cloud as a specific transgression such as dishonesty, breaking the Sabbath day, or not keeping the Word of Wisdom. Clarify again that Christ has never left us, but our bad choices keep us from experiencing the love and light he offers.

Choral Reading: Invite the children to read the verse printed on the lineboard.

Object Lesson: Display the plant. Point out that it is yellowed and wilting. Explain that it is planted in good rich soil, that it got plenty of water, that you even talked to it, but it is still beginning to die. The only thing this plant didn't get is sunshine. Plants and other living things need sunshine to be healthy and survive. We need the light of Christ just as much as this plant needed the sunlight. If we transgress and block his light we will find ourselves in as serious a condition as the plant.

Singing Time Suggestions

"Teach Me to Walk in the Light," 177
"Shine On," 144

Conclusion

Introduce your guest. Have him or her share a personal experience and testimony illustrating the importance of the light of Christ.

Wisdom

Purpose

To teach the children that wisdom is more than knowing what is right. It is doing what is right.

Materials Needed

Chalk, chalkboard, eraser.

Preparation

Print the following verses on slips of paper: "Happy is the man that findeth wisdom" (Proverbs 3:13), "For wisdom is better than rubies" (Proverbs 8:11), "How much better is it to get wisdom than gold!" (Proverbs 16:16), "Wisdom is better than strength" (Ecclesiastes 9:16).

Print the entire verse of Alma 37:35 on a lineboard. ("O, remember, my son, and learn wisdom in thy youth; yea, learn in thy youth to keep the commandments of God.")

Print the entire alphabet across your chalkboard. Underneath each letter, number from 1 to 26. This is your alphabet code. Using this code the children should decipher: 23 – 9 – 19 – 4 – 15 – 13.

Prepare to tell "Johnny."

Application

Story: "Johnny"

Johnny was ten years old. He was a smart boy. But that didn't keep him out of trouble. In fact Johnny seemed to look for trouble. One summer day he saw the old, dead, apple tree in the backyard. Dad hadn't had time to cut it down yet, and he warned Johnny not to climb in it because the wood was weak and rotten. But that day Johnny just had to see for himself. So he climbed up into the tree and onto a shaky branch. Sure enough there was a big crack! Johnny crashed to the ground and broke his leg! He spent the rest of the summer in a hot, heavy cast.

Another time Johnny saw a stray cat in his backyard. Mother had taught him to stay away from strange animals because they could hurt him. But Johnny just wanted to know for himself. It took quite a bit of time to corner the cat by the shed. Slowly he moved towards the trapped animal. He was almost ready to grab the cat when it pounced right on him. Johnny screamed and scared the cat even more. By the time he and the cat managed to get apart Johnny had a lot of scratches.

On the first day of the new school year, Johnny dressed in his new clothes and shoes. As he waited for the bus he saw his baseball in the middle of the garden. It had rained very hard the night before. Johnny knew the garden was probably muddy. But once again, he just had to find out for himself. He tried to step lightly, but after a couple of steps, he sunk deep into the oozing mud. By the time he managed to pull himself out his new clothes and shoes were caked with mud. Johnny would have to wear his older clothes to school that day.

Game: Explain to the children that Johnny was a smart boy. He was brave, strong, and adventurous. But there was one thing Johnny didn't have. Challenge the group to figure out what it was. Refer them to the game you have prepared on the board. Invite them to crack the code. After they have discovered the answer conduct a brief discussion.

Discussion: Ask: did Johnny know those things were wrong to do? (Yes.) He ignored the things he had been taught and did what he wanted to do. That shows us that Johnny lacked wisdom. Explain that wisdom is displayed when you use the knowledge you have to help you make good choices.

Scripture Reading: Pass out the four scripture slips to children in your group. Have them each read their verse out loud. After each verse is read ask the children what they learned about wisdom from that scripture.

Singing Time Suggestions

"Seek the Lord Early," 108
"Choose the Right Way," 160

Conclusion

Display the lineboard and read the verse to your group. Explain that wisdom is a wonderful treasure. Heavenly Father desires of us to learn how to be wise.

Making Reusable Visuals

Making Reusable Visuals

Reusable visual aids are not a new idea and they are easy to make. For many years people have been using them effectively in family or Church teaching situations.

The purpose of a reusable visual is to save time and money while producing a quality visual aid. To be most effective, reusable visual aids must be simple enough to fit a variety of circumstances or subjects.

The authors' preference in marking the reusable visuals has been a transparency marker, with a damp cloth for cleanup. However, dry erase markers work well on most laminations. It is a matter of preference. We do recommend trying your marker on a corner first. (Both transparency and dry erase markers are available at most stationery supply stores and at Church distribution centers.) Also, though we have given specific measurements for each reusable visual, you may want to adjust these measurements according to your specific needs.

The reusable visuals mentioned in this section (excepting the *Celebration Board*) have been used throughout the lesson activities section. After you have made a few reusable visuals, allow creativity to take over. Anytime you make a visual aid, ask yourself, "How can I make this reusable?" Ideas for reusable visuals are limitless.

Lineboard

This versatile visual is used for anything from writing a scripture or quote, to drawing stick figures, to a "chalkboard" discussion.

Materials Needed: Poster board, pencil, ruler, marker, good eraser.

1. Using the ruler and pencil, measure in two inches from the outside edges of the poster board. This will determine your border.

2. Carefully trace or mark over the penciled border with marker. This finishes the border.

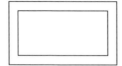

3. Use the ruler and pencil to mark lines about two inches apart inside the border. The lines may be horizontal or vertical. These will be your lettering guides.

4. Turn the poster board over and repeat steps one and two or use an alternate border (see below).
5. Use your ruler and pencil to mark lines 1 1/2 inches apart inside the border.
6. Have your new lineboard laminated. Now your project is completed!

Ideas for Alternate Lineboard Boarders: (1) Use the basic line border, but in one corner place a 5 x 7 picture of the Savior, children being reverent, a family, etc. (2) Use large or small stickers on or around the line border for added color. (3) Use bright colored markers to make a double- or triple-line border. (4) Draw shapes, swirls, flowers, or other designs in the border area. Color with bright markers or crayons. (5) Be creative and try your own.

Wordstrips

Instead of constantly cutting out paper strips for important words, use the reusable wordstrips and a transparency marker. When you're done, simply erase the words and save the strips for your next lesson.

Materials Needed: Poster board, pencil, ruler.

1. With the ruler and pencil, divide the strips (horizontal or vertical). These will be your wordstrips.
2. Using the ruler and pencil, mark a two-inch width in the center of each wordstrip. This is your lettering guide.

3. Cut apart the wordstrips and laminate them. Your wordstrips are now ready to use.

Wordshapes

Wordshapes are probably the most versatile reusable visual. Use them for idea emphasis, as wordstrips, as clues, or as a choosing game.

Materials Needed: Poster board (colored poster board is excellent), pencil, shape stencil, ruler, markers.

1. Divide the poster board into eleven-inch by nine-inch squares. Each poster board will make six visual squares.
2. Using a marker, draw your simple design (circle, star, heart, etc.) on the visual square. These are your shapes.
3. Mark every design with a pencil lettering guide. (See *Lineboard*, step 3.)
4. Cut out each design and laminate.

Celebration Board

This wonderful reusable visual helps you celebrate special occasions. Use if for birthdays, baptisms, advancements, or for any other achievement you wish to acknowledge.

Materials Needed: Poster board, pencil, ruler, markers, glue, confetti (confetti can be made by using a hole punch on bright colored paper).

1. Using the ruler and pencil, measure in 1 1/2 inches from the outside edges of the board. This will be your border.
2. Trace or mark over the penciled line using the marker. This will finish your border.
3. Using any kind of printing or ready-made lettering, place a heading on the top of the board. For example: "Happy Birthday," "Celebrate With Us," "Congratulations," "It's a Special Day," etc.
4. Use the ruler and pencil to mark lines about two inches apart under the heading. These are your lettering guides.

5. Apply small dots of glue on your poster board. These may be placed in the lettering area, in the border, or all over the board. Press the pieces of confetti onto the glue dots.
6. Repeat steps one to five on the reverse side. To offer variety on side two, draw squiggle streamers or balloons to replace the confetti.
7. Laminate your celebration board.

Thermometer Chart

The thermometer chart is a great motivational tool. Children watch the temperature on the thermometer rise as their participation or mastery increases. It works well for singing time, brainstorming sessions, and much more.

Materials Needed: White poster board, pencil, ruler, compass, black marker.

1. Use your ruler and pencil to mark two lines lengthwise on your poster board. These lines should be two inches apart in the center of the poster board. Begin the lines four inches from the top and finish them four inches from the bottom.
2. Use a compass to fashion a circular-shaped bulb at the bottom of the thermometer. Finish by drawing a short straight line across the top of the two lines.
3. Using a black marker, trace or mark over the penciled lines. This will form the basic design of the thermometer.
4. With the ruler and pencil, draw horizontal lines to divide the thermometer into several parts. These will be your guides to "make the temperature rise."
5. Laminate your thermometer chart. Use a red transparency marker to indicate the temperature. A damp cloth will erase as necessary.

Music Time Ideas

Music Time Ideas

Music is one of the most challenging yet rewarding parts of any sharing or family time. Helping children enjoy singing takes preparation, enthusiasm, prayer, and a willing attitude. Music can be fun to learn and to sing!

Because music is such an important part of any Primary or family program, several musical "games" and ideas have been included in this section. These cannot take the place of your own personal appreciation for music—they are only ideas to be used in teaching that appreciation. To begin with, here are some tips that will make any singing activity more effective:

1. Always introduce your song with positive comment. If you tell the children that the song is hard, too high, or a "have to," they will find it more difficult to learn and consequently less enjoyable.
2. Louder is *not* always better. A good rule to go by is "Never louder than lovely." Consider your group and help them understand the difference.
3. A child's voice is different from an adult's. Just because a song is too high for an adult does not mean it is too high for most children.
4. Try to keep any activities group-oriented. Singling out individuals for any reason can cause hurt feelings, embarrassment, or feelings of rejection.
5. Consider the purpose. Are you teaching words and notes, or the feeling and spirit of the song?
6. Love each child. Children pick up feelings readily and know if you love them or consider them as a challenge to be overcome.
7. Coordinate your efforts. Always let your pianist know what you will be doing. Be sure to counsel with your leaders about needs and goals and coordinate lesson themes whenever possible.
8. Pray continually for guidance from the Spirit. Music has the ability to teach concepts and reach individuals in a very special way.

Alternating Groups

This activity requires the following three picture puppets: a boy, a girl, and an adult. They can be made by mounting the appropriate pictures on Popsicle sticks. This type of puppet allows you to hold one, two, or three puppets at the same time.

Explain to the group that each puppet represents whose turn it is to sing. Select a familiar song and begin. Alternate the picture puppets throughout the song. Display them singly or in any combination of two or three. Try not to rotate the puppets too quickly as it can confuse the children.

Erase the Word

Prior to singing time, write on the chalkboard the words to a song. Display the chalkboard to your group and sing the song. Have one of the children take the eraser and erase one word from the song. Sing the song again. This time the children will have to remember the missing word. Continue this process several times, having the children fill in the blanks as they sing. This is especially helpful in teaching new songs.

Guess the Subject

On a lineboard, mount an example of your subject. For instance, write the word "pioneer" on your lineboard or have a picture of pioneers. Write the titles of applicable songs on four to six wordshapes. Cover the subject with the wordshapes. Have a child come forward and choose one of the wordshapes. Sing the song listed on the wordshape and, if time permits, briefly give a thought about what the song teaches. Repeat until all the songs have been chosen.

When the subject is completely uncovered, ask the children to guess what all the songs have been about.

Hot and Cold

Have a selected child briefly step out of the room. Hide an object of your choosing in the room. As the child returns lead the group in a song. The children will sing more loudly as the child gets closer to the hidden object and will sing more quietly when he is further away. This continues until the object is found. Remember, "Never louder than lovely."

Mixed Phrases

Select a song. Write each line or phrase of the song onto a separate wordstrip. Place the wordstrips in incorrect order on the display area.

Ask a child to come forward and choose the first phrase of the song. Read it to the children or have them read it with you. Post it as first on your display area. Repeat until the children have put all of the wordstrips in the correct order. Now sing the song.

Music Basket

Fill a basket with several seasonal items—for example, fruit, plastic eggs, flowers, styrofoam balls (snowballs), etc. Tape the name of a song on each item.

Have a child come forward and choose a "song." Repeat until all the songs have been chosen. This is perfect for a review of already learned music.

Stop and Go

Prepare a red sign labeled "stop" and a green sign labeled "go." Explain to your group that when you display the "go" sign they should sing. When the "stop" sign is displayed they should hum. Select a familiar song and begin singing. Alternate the signs throughout the song. Be careful not to switch them too often, as this detracts from the song.

Thermometer Chart

Use the thermometer chart described in the reusable visuals section for this activity. Display the chart to your group and explain that the object of the activity is to get the thermometer to reach the boiling point. The temperature will rise according to how well they participate. Use a red transparency marker to fill in the thermometer as the children sing each song.

This activity can also be used to encourage children to learn the words to a new song. The temperature will increase as they master the song.

What's the Song?

Ask the pianist to play the first three notes of a preselected song. Ask the children to guess the name of the song. If they cannot, play the first six notes of that same song and ask them to guess again. If they are still not able to name the song, have the pianist play the first nine notes.

When the song is finally named, have the children sing that song. Continue to do this until all the preselected songs have been sung.

What's the Word?

Write the words to a song on the chalkboard. Decide on several key words throughout the song and erase them.

Present the song to the children and tell them that some important words are missing. Ask them to tell you what they are. Depending upon the age of your group, you may write in the words as they tell you, or the children can write them in.

Similarly, instead of erasing words, you can insert pictures for words. You might use an eye for *I*, a picture of Jesus for the word *Jesus*, a heart for *love*, etc.